Large Marbles:
- The Matron 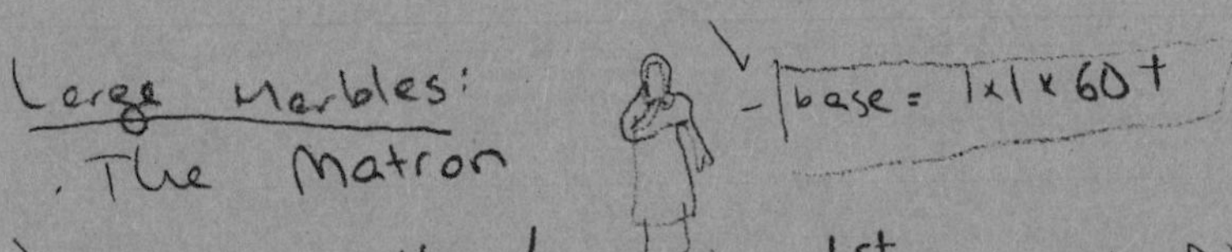 — base = 1×1×60+
- 3 men standing in 1st room :. Notable Roman
  3 × bases = 70×70×60+

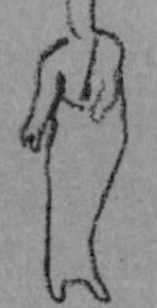

- Giovinetto orante. 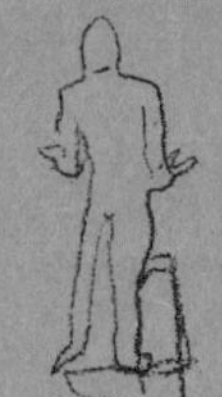
  Bases — 70×70×50+

. Aeschines 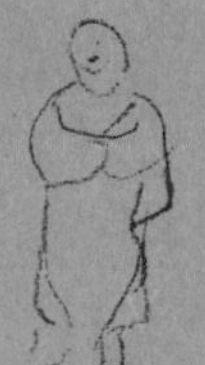   . Homer

- Fountein
  w/ cowheads   base 1×1m × 60+

Large Bronzes:
- Hermes at Rest 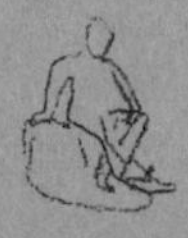
  2× bases: 150×100×50+

- Sleeping Satyr 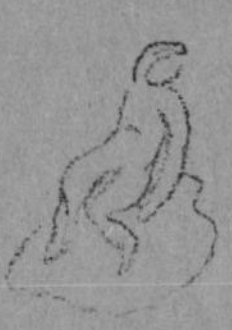

- Fawns ×2 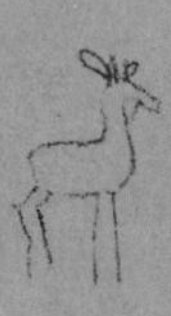
  2×bases: 130×50 × 50+

- Dancers × 3 —
  3 × bases 60×60 × 50+

- Peplophoros
  or
  Hypermnestra 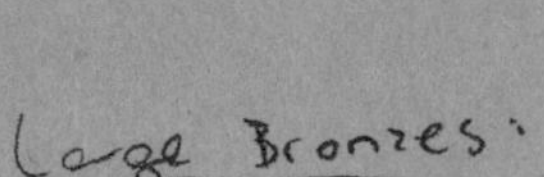
  base 150×50×60+

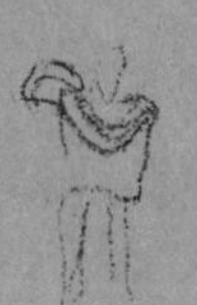
getting
dressed

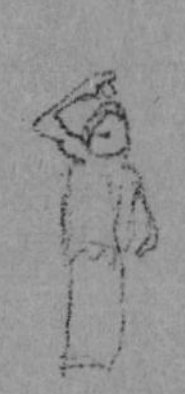
relaxed
top head pt.

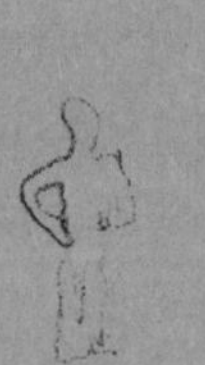
inviter

Busts Room 1
Marble: Herm of 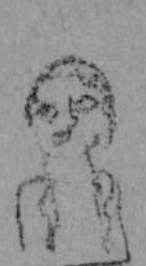
           Hercules

Black bases
±10 ×40×40

Bronze (by windows)

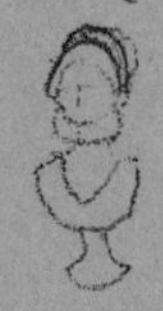
Archytas

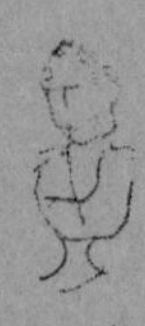
Heraclitus

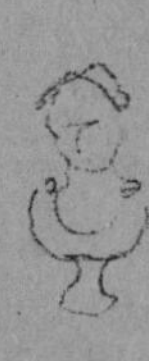
Young
Commander

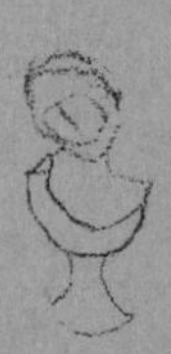
Democritus

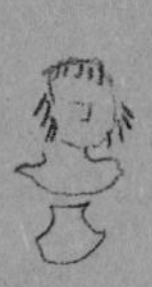
Ptolomy
Apion

OROGENESI

Juliana Cerqueira Leite

TROLLEY

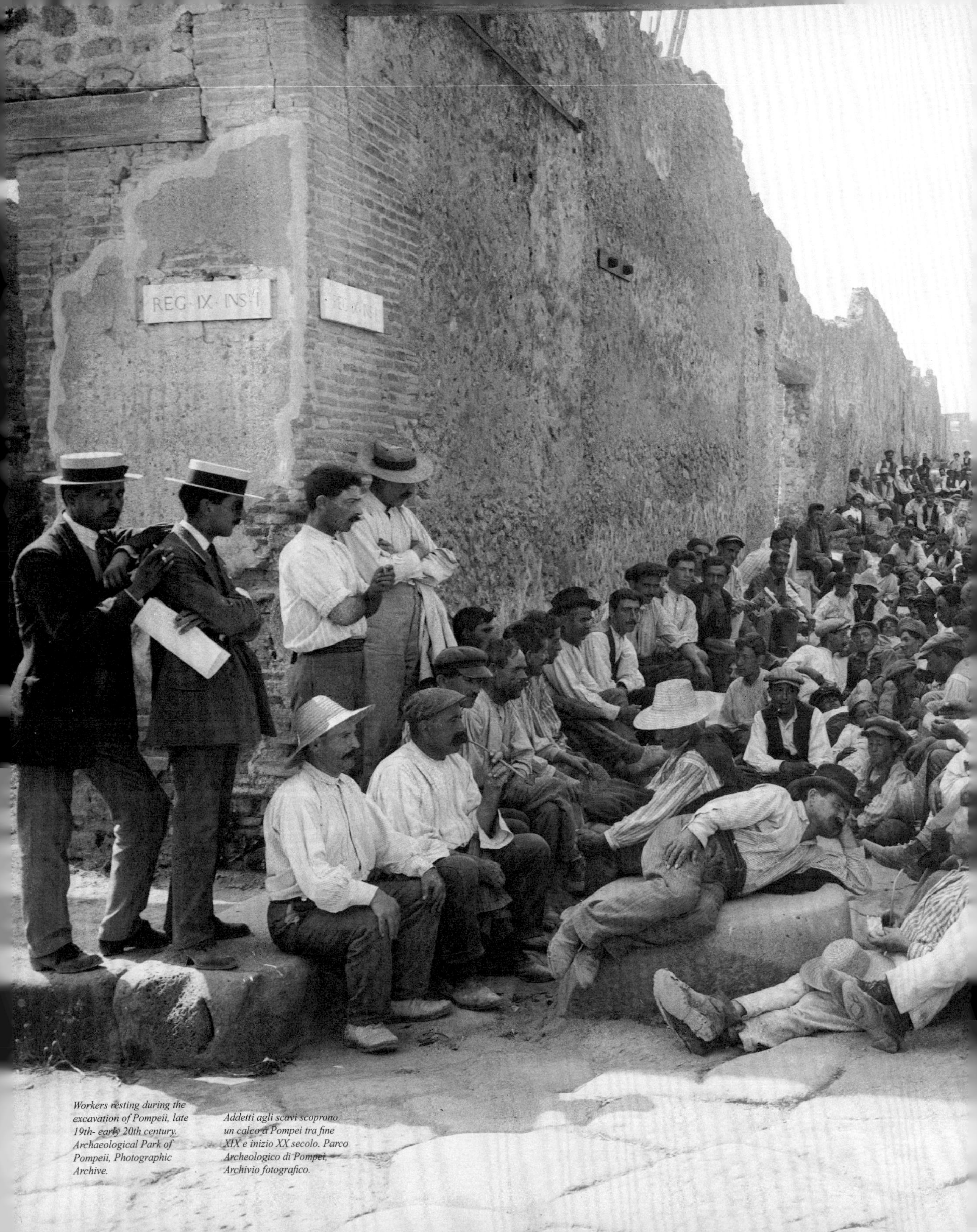

Workers resting during the excavation of Pompeii, late 19th- early 20th century. Archaeological Park of Pompeii, Photographic Archive.

Addetti agli scavi scoprono un calco a Pompei tra fine XIX e inizio XX secolo. Parco Archeologico di Pompei, Archivio fotografico.

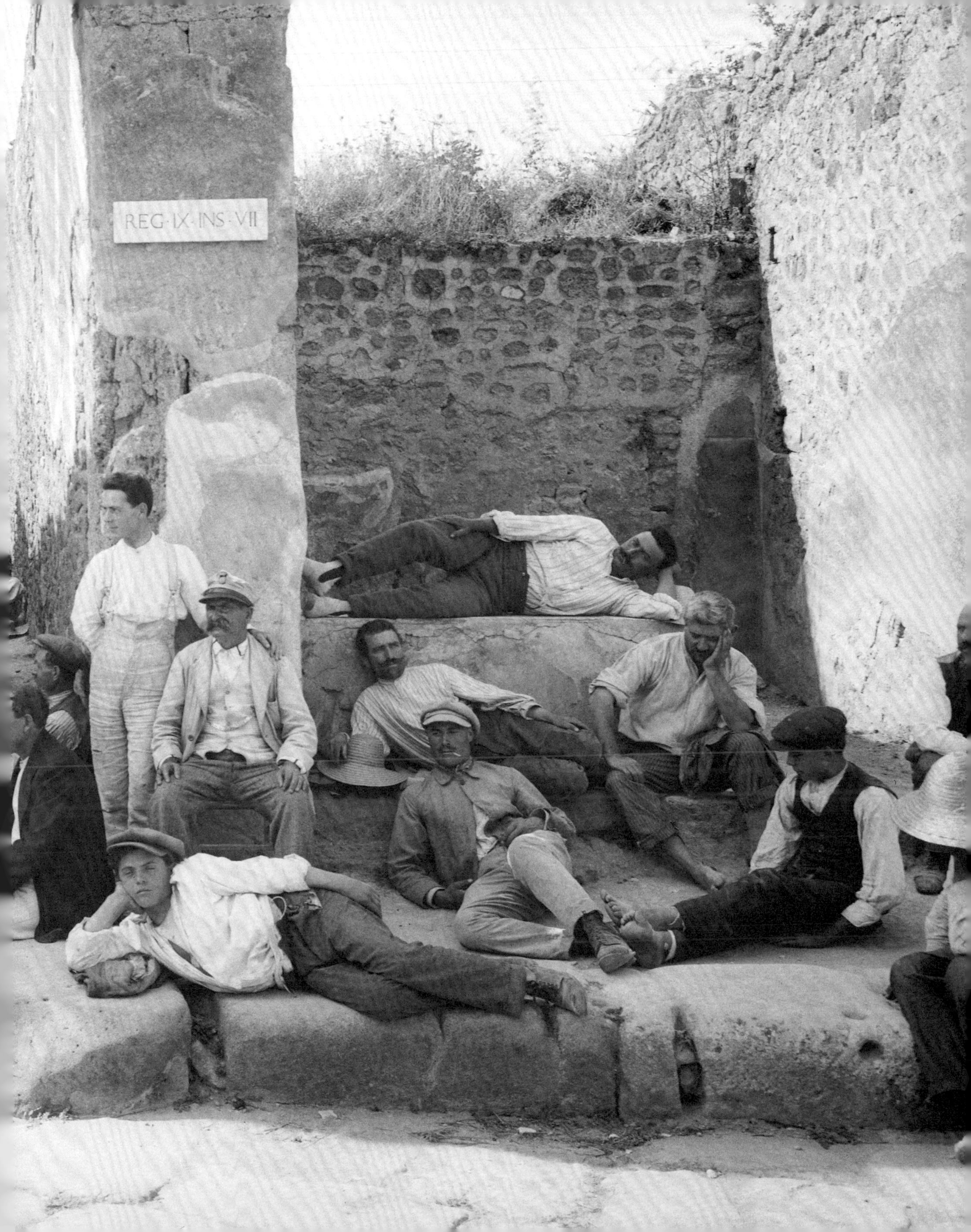
REG · IX · INS · VII

Mario Codognato

*I think you always have to find where the
boundary is in relation to the context in order
to be able to kind of articulate how you want
the space to interact with the viewer.*

Richard Serra

*When you do dance, I wish you
A wave o' th' sea, that you might ever do
Nothing but that*

William Shakespeare.
The Winter's Tale (IV,iv, 159-161).

In geology, the term orogenesis (which comes from
the Ancient Greek words ὄρος = mountain + γένεσις
= origin) is used to indicate the process of the creation
of elevations in nature. The word refers to *orogens*, the
result of tectonic modifications in which some plates
collide or are pushed over others, creating a mountain
range. This process can be an emblematic metaphor
for artistic practice, and in particular for sculpture and
its history, which has always accompanied the human
odyssey on this Earth. The material/the mountain/
the shape/the sculpture is modified through collisions
and erosion, as is life. Seemingly static and eternal,
it is, in fact, the result of countless movements,
chances, concurrent causes, plans, variables and
stratifications. Stratification is the essence of every
artistic production. Every piece collects and contains
experience acquired from the past; archetypes that
follow human history, contradictions of the present,
previsions for the future, social constructs, and the
artist's own experience.

"Orogenesis" is also the title of the project that
Juliana Cerqueira Leite is presenting at the National
Archaeological Museum in Naples, one of the most
ancient and prestigious institutions for Greek and
Roman art worldwide. The museum's extraordinary
heritage is mainly composed of the Farnese Collection
from classical Rome and of artefacts found during
the excavations of the buried cities of Herculaneum
and Pompeii in the Vesuvian area. Therefore, in the
collective imagination, sculptures such as the *Farnese
Bull* and the *Venus Callipyge* coexist together with the

fuggiaschi pompeiani (Pompeian fugiti es). The latter
are the cast bodies of the victims seeking safety from
the Vesuvius eruption in 79 AD, whose tragic images
are juxtaposed with the harmony and virtuosity of
the classical sculptures, the idealised *Venus*, their
harmonious physicality in conflict with the tension
of the twisted body of the fugitive, extended in a
desperate, extreme acceleration.

The latter's dynamics are the starting point of the
analysis carried out by Cerqueira Leite's project.
The cast bodies, called *calchi*, have been obtained by
following the Fiorelli method. This technique consists
of using liquid plaster to fill the empty spaces left by the
bodies in the layer of solidified ash, where their forms
had been conserved in tact. Thanks to this procedure,
it is now possible to see the features of these ancient
bodies and faces, still conserving the tragic pain of their
last living moments.

Cerqueira Leite was inspired also by Aby Warburg's
Bilderatlas Mnemosyne, a system that puts together
images nfrom different fields and inspects iconographic
and literary sources, as well as the cultural and
historical circumstances that lead to artistic creation.s
In particular, Cerqueira Leite compares images of the
fugitives with archival photographs of NASA space
missions and of choreographer Martha Graham's
legendary performances. This creates a visual and
conceptual short-circuit that has at its core the human
body, which is also the foundation of the sculpture in
all its forms and negations.

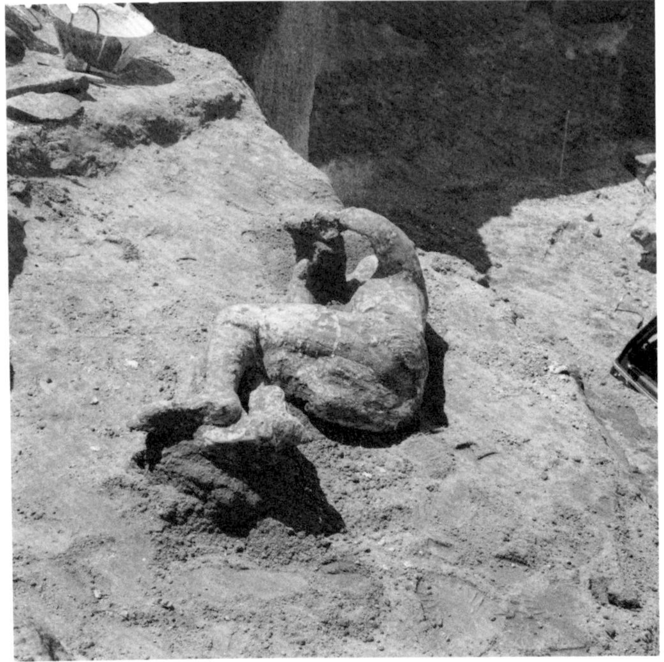

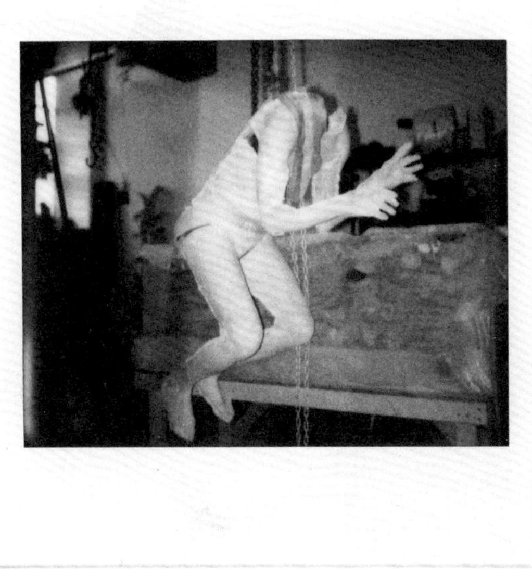

The movements in zero gravity that astronauts have
to execute during a mission create an extreme and
radical body language, foreign to the human sphere,
as immortalised in Stanley Kubrick's *2001: A Space
Odyssey*. In zero gravity, the body fluids, which are no
longer pulled downwards, are spread homogeneously
throughout the body. Muscles would tend to atrophy
without any physical efforts to keep them exercised,
so to maintain their muscular tone the astronauts train
every day with treadmills or elastic bands, pushing
and pulling their legs and arms, in order to partially
recreate the efforts due to gravity. In a spaceship, or
a space station, up and down do not exist. There is no
difference between the ceiling and the floor. The body
loses any usual reference point. As the artist points out,
the NBP (Neutral Body Posture) defined by NASA as
the standard pose of human body in absence of gravity,
is unbelievably similar to the position of the fugitives'
calchi, due to the fact that the body in space suffers from
anatomical constraints that are comparable to those
forming the pugilistic attitude. The contracting muscles
are stronger, causing the joints to bend involuntarily
once the counter strength of gravity is absent.

In Martha Graham's extraordinary choreographic
work, these contractions happen through a complex
process. Yuriko, one of Graham's closest collaborators,
describes it this way:
"The sculptured contraction is my name for this
movement, because when Martha first gave it to us she
said that we should feel like a piece of sculpture with
holes, such as in a Henry Moore sculpture. That is, we
should have the feeling of air going through the holes
in our bones. […] But here is the original movement:
standing on the right leg, knees parallel, lift the left leg
into a side attitude along the same line as in the right
supporting leg. The left knee is only slightly bent and
the right is demi-plié. A contraction begins on the left
side and travels into the back or sit bones, with the
pelvis parallel to the floor, and the contraction ends
on the right hip.

The position of the arm: right arm bent ad in front of
the body. The left arm stretches to the side; the head
is turned slightly to the right. Martha said we should
visualize air going through holes in our bones and
ending in a reach through to the sky from the elbow."[1]

Sculptured contractions are what Cerqueira Leite has
produced for her show at the Archeological Museum.
Extreme bodies in extreme positions and conditions
contract in front of our eyes and offer a privileged
reading, but they also hold, like archaeological
artefacts, a layered interpretation that unfolds the past.
History and contemporaneity, the melancholy for lost
time, fragmentation of objects and of one's self, and
metaphors for existence, are all present and contracted
in a movement that is not only physical, but embracing
life and language in all of their contradictions.

[1] Martha Graham: the evolution of her dance theory and training, [compiled
by] Marian Horosko, Gainesville: University Press of Florida, 1991.

Fig. 1
Calchi, or plaster cast
body produced during
the excavation of
Pompeii. c. 1863-1940

Fig. 2
Work in progress:
Calcify, 2019,
Brooklyn studio.

Mario Codognato

*Penso che devi sempre trovare dove il confine è
in relazione con il contesto per essere in grado
di articolare il modo in cui vuoi che lo spazio
interagisca con lo spettatore.*
Richard Serra

*Quando balli, ti auguro
Un'onda del mare, che potresti mai fare
Nient'altro che quello*
William Shakespeare.
The Winter's Tale (IV, iv, 159-161).

Alla voce Orogenesi (dal greco ὄρος = rilievo, montagna
+ γένεσις = origine, causa produttiva) il dizionario
indica che in geologia è il processo di formazione di un
qualsiasi rilievo. Nel linguaggio geologico, il termine
si riferisce alla formazione degli *orogeni*, derivanti da
masse rocciose che hanno subito una deformazione
tettonica per prevalenza di spinte laterali, arrivando
quindi ad impilarsi creando una catena montuosa. Tale
processo potrebbe significare una potente metafora
per la prassi dell'arte ed in particolare della scultura,
e la sua storia che accompagna in ogni dove l'odissea
dell'umanità sulla Terra. La materia/la montagna/la
forma/la scultura è modificata attraverso collisioni ed
erosioni, come la vita. Sembra statica ed eterna, ma in
realtà è il frutto di innumerevoli movimenti, casualità,
concause, pianificazioni, variabili e stratificazioni.

La stratificazione è anche l'essenza di ogni produzione
artistica, che inevitabilmente raccoglie e coagula le
esperienze del passato, gli archetipi che si sono susseguiti
nella storia dell'umano, le contraddizioni del presente,
le proiezioni del futuro, i condizionamenti della società
e le esperienze soggettive dell'artista.

Orogenesi è anche il titolo del progetto di Juliana
Cerqueira Leite al Museo Archeologico Nazionale
di Napoli, uno dei più antichi ed importanti al
mondo per l'arte greco-romana. La sua straordinaria
collezione è principalmente costituita dalla raccolta
Farnese proveniente da Roma e dai reperti scavati
nella aerea vesuviana nelle città sepolte di Ercolano
e Pompei. Nell'immaginario collettivo convivono

perciò l'armonia e il virtuosismo del Toro Farnese e
della Venere Callipigia con l'immagine tragicamente
realistica dei celebri *fuggiaschi pompeiani*, i calchi
delle vittime dell'eruzione del 79 d.C. mentre cercavano
scampo dalla violenza del Vesuvio. Il corpo idealizzato
ed armonico della Venere in collisone visiva con la
tensione e la torsione del corpo del fuggiasco proteso
ad un'accelerazione disperata ed estrema. La dinamica
e le dinamiche di quest'ultimo sono il fulcro e il punto
di partenza dell'analisi alla base del progetto della
Cerquira Leite. Questi calchi sono stati ottenuti con
il metodo Fiorelli, che consiste nel versare del gesso
liquido nella cavità lasciata dal corpo nello strato di
cenere solidificata che ne ha conservato intatta la forma.
Grazie a questo procedimento, possiamo ancora oggi
vedere le fattezze dei corpi e dei volti che conservano
la drammaticità del dolore provato nell'ultimo momento
della loro vita.

Seguendo un sistema ispirato al *Bilderatlas Mnemosyne*
di Aby Warburg, nel quale attraverso l'accostamento di
immagini di varie provenienze, si compie un'indagine a
tutto campo sulla cultura occidentale, attraverso l'esame
delle fonti iconografiche e letterarie e un'analisi delle
circostanze storiche e culturali della creazione artistica,
Cerquira Leite accosta le immagini dei fuggiaschi a
immagini di repertorio delle spedizioni spaziali della
NASA e alle leggendarie performance della coreografa
Martha Graham, creando un cortocircuito visivo e
concettuale che ha come epicentro il corpo umano,
a sua volta la base della scultura in tutte le sue forme
e negazioni. I movimenti in assenza di gravità che gli

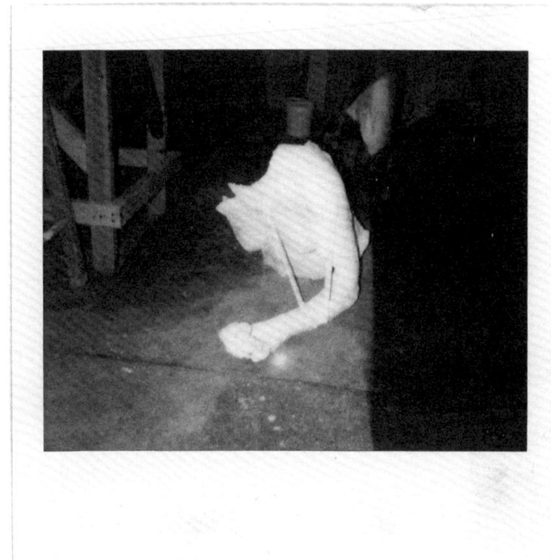

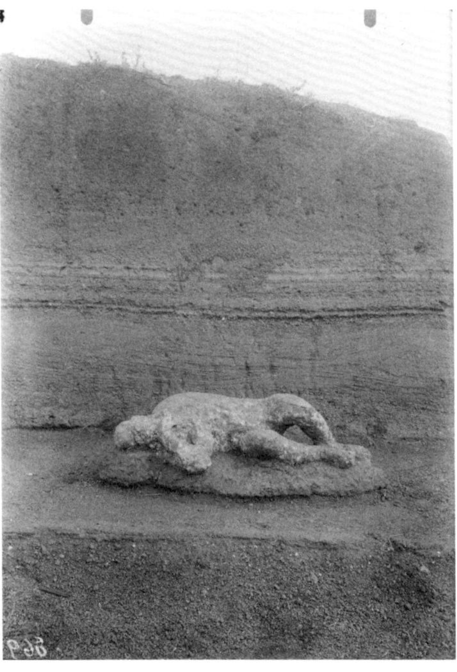

astronauti devono compiere durante le missioni spaziali danno vita a un linguaggio corporeo estremo e radicale, come estraneo all'ambito umano, e come immortalati in *2001: Odissea Nello Spazio* di Stanley Kubrick. In assenza di gravità infatti i liquidi dell'organismo, non più attratti verso il basso, si distribuiscono in modo pressoché omogeneo in ogni distretto corporeo. I muscoli tenderebbero all'atrofia perché non ci sono più sforzi fisici da fare che li terrebbero allenati. Per mantenere il proprio tono muscolare gli astronauti devono eseguire giornalmente esercizi con tappeti rullanti o con elastici: allontanando e avvicinando le braccia e le gambe ricreano in parte lo sforzo che farebbero in presenza di gravità. In una navetta o in una stazione spaziale non esiste sopra o sotto. Non c'è alcuna differenza fra soffitto e pavimento. Il corpo perde ogni punto di riferimento abituale. Come puntualizza l'artista stessa: la NBP (posa del corpo neutro) che la NASA ha determinato per il corpo umano a gravità zero è incredibilmente simile alla posa dei calchi dei fuggiaschi perché il corpo nello spazio soffre delle stesse costrizioni anatomiche che causano questa posa pugilistica. I muscoli contraenti sono più forti, quindi le articolazioni si piegano naturalmente quando si elimina la controforza della gravità, diventa un gesto involontario. Nella straordinaria opera coreografica di Martha Graham, queste contrazioni avvengono attraverso un complesso e deliberato processo. Yuriko, una delle più strette collaboratrici della Graham la descrive così: "Contrazione scultorea è il nome che ho dato a questo movimento, perché quando Martha ce lo ha insegnato la prima volta ci ha detto che avremmo dovuto provare a sentirci come una scultura con dei buchi, come una scultura di Henry Moore. Cioè, dovevamo avere la sensazione che l'aria passasse attraverso i fori nelle nostre ossa…. In piedi sulla gamba destra, le ginocchia parallele, sollevando la gamba sinistra in un atteggiamento laterale lungo la stessa linea della gamba destra di supporto. Il ginocchio sinistro è solo leggermente piegato e il destro è in demi-plié. Una contrazione inizia sul lato sinistro e si sposta nella parte posteriore, con il bacino parallelo al pavimento, e la contrazione termina sul fianco destro. La posizione del braccio: braccio destro piegato e davanti al corpo. Il braccio sinistro si estende lateralmente; la testa è girata leggermente a destra. Martha ha detto che dovremmo visualizzare l'aria che passa attraverso i buchi nelle nostre ossa e che termina nella direzione del cielo dal gomito."

Contrazioni scultoree sono in definitiva le opere che Juliana Cerqueira Leite ha prodotto per la sua mostra al Museo Archeologico. Corpi estremi in posizioni e condizioni estreme si contraggono allo sguardo e ad una lettura univoca o privilegiata, ma si abbandonano, come i reperti archeologici, a una lettura stratificata nel tempo e dal tempo. C'è la storia, c'è la contemporaneità, c'è la melanconia del tempo perduto, c'è la frammentazione degli oggetti e dell'essere, c'è la metafora dell'esistenza, contratta in un movimento e in una posa che non è solo fisica, ma che abbraccia la vita ed il linguaggio in tutte le loro contraddizioni.

1. Martha Graham: the evolution of her dance theory and training, [compiled by] Marian Horosko, Gainesville: University Press of Florida, 1991.

Dehlia Hannah & Nadim Samman

DH__   When tectonic plates collide, the lateral pressure either forces surface material upwards along both sides of the fault line, forming mountain ranges, or causes one of the plates to buckle beneath the other, creating volcanoes. This process is termed orogenesis. Earthquakes and fiery mountains have always captured the cultural imagination, figuring prominently in origin myths, as a metaphor for political upheaval and psychological turmoil. Vesuvius is a paradigmatic case of a volcano that has destroyed and yet preserved a world. Perhaps it has even been creative, in terms of its cultural significance. As a sculptor, Leite often gives solid form to gestures and dynamic motions, such as climbing or reaching. Invoking the birth of mountains, the title of this exhibition proposes analogies between geologic configurations of matter and postures assumed by the human body.

NS__   In many of her works Leite effects female nudes in plaster. This choice of medium engages particular symbolic and art historical tropes: plaster is a neo-classical material, and so we are immediately in the discursive realm of *how* a body should be represented. For the belle arti, classical sculptures of the sort housed in the National Archaeological Museum were the best examples. Artifacts such as the Farnese marbles, and those housed in the Villa dei Papyri, were *object lessons*. In many academies, plaster casts of such sculptures were used as teaching models—to draw from, etc. Striving for a one-to-one relation to classical triumphs (in art, and perhaps even subjectivity) the academicians' sought to fix, quite literally, upon the best—through a profusion of plaster copies. Through deployment of this indexical material, plaster, a certain aspect of academic art was

a monument to ancient monumental sculpture and its bodies. But how could it ever achieve its task?

Consider the *calchi*. Human bodies buried under the ashes at Pompeii existed just long enough for negative casts to be made by natural accident. Later, these casts were refilled by human agency. The *calchi* are positive plaster casts of the negative space left by the bodies. Leite's project invites one to speculate about the political function of the *calchi* as monumental sculptures of a sort (or sculpture-relics). Indulging this meditation, we must ask if they are merely monuments to the idiosyncratic life of particular people, and the tragedy that befell the town of Pompeii, *or* if they operate in another way. In the context of this exhibition, might they, for instance, support some kind of spiritual/metaphysical proposition in relation to the sculptural figures recovered from the same site? One looks to Juliana's sculptures as conceptual mediators between the *calchi* and the classical sculptures of the Villa dei Papiri. But they seem to relate to more than that too…

DH__   . It is interesting to consider how this ancient world has been conjured for the modern imagination. The excavation of Pompeii began in the mid-eighteenth century, fueling an obsession with antiquity (and antiquities) that drew elite travelers on the Grand Tour over the Alps to Rome, and then further south to Naples. This was a journey on which new aesthetic categories were born. Once viewed as ugly and dangerous obstacles on the route to the beauties of Italy, mountains became sublime.[1] Broken statues became transports for the imagination for the Romantics. In the rubble, poets and philosophers found keys to

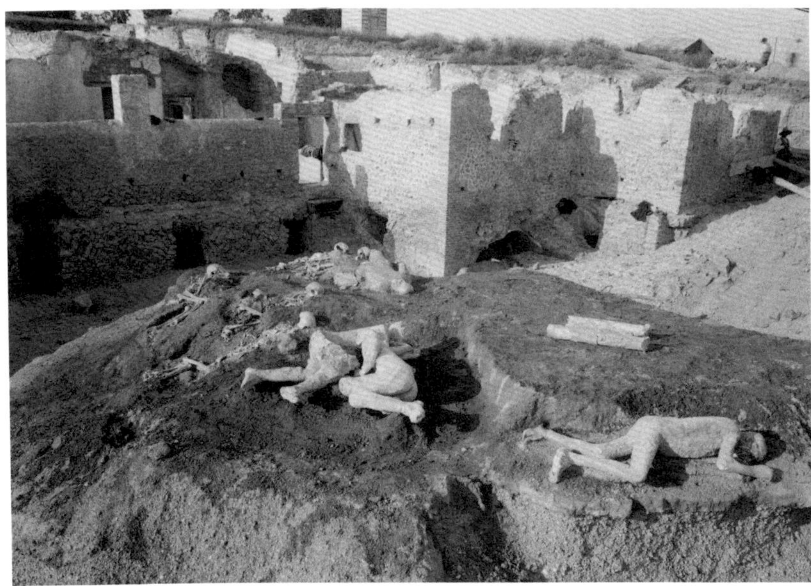

the grandeur of a lost past, tokens of mourning for Modernity's secular fall from an ancient state of grace. From a piece of a broken classical sculpture (a hand; a foot) one might extrapolate to the complete figure. This imaginative operation relies on the underlying logic of an idealized body, whose perfect sculptural representation is implied by any given element. Ultimately the fragment becames an aesthetic form in its own right, and works of art and literature are created 'unfinished.'

As you observe, Leite's project brings the relic into dialogue with classical sculpture via the evidentiary artifact of archaeological excavation. If fragments are transports for the imagination, relics are transports for the soul—a hair, a fingernail, a shred of clothing, a bone from the foot of a saint, anchors a spiritual presence within historical time. While engaging with the *calchi* as aesthetic forms, Leite simultaneously offers them up as indices of profane bodies. The implication is that, like religious relics, the cachi contain fragments of a life, albeit an everyday life. A fragment of a classical sculpture is not just a piece of a figure that is beautiful in its formal proportions. It offers a glimpse of a lifeworld in which the gods were present and taken to inhere substantively within such artifacts. Leite returns to Pompeii to excavate other aesthetic logics using new bodily and material practices.

NS__   Staying with material politics—the link between plaster and the relic is the death mask. In the 'enlightened' state that emerged in eighteenth-century France, archaic religiosity and the modern came together in this quasi-sculptural practice. Recall how Madame Tussaud's first business was casting severed heads that fell from the guillotine. Certain heroes (ordained by the not entirely *ancient* regime of Christian monarchy) had to be torn down before a post-revolutionary Neo-Classicism could take hold in the arts, with the reliquary bridging the gap between art *per se* and the world as an aesthetic project. After toppling the old statues, and fragmenting so many real bodies, plaster casts of faces emerge as key symptoms of a post-revolutionary body. This said, we should note that such positive quasi-monuments, taken from negative casts, are made from wax, something even more soft and fragile than plaster—something closer to liquid. Certainly, this is a suggestive metaphor for modern politics—that reality is infinitely malleable: sculptable.

DH__   I am reminded of Linda Nochlin's argument that, after the iconic use of the guillotine during the French Revolution, the fragment is always accompanied by the promise—and the threat—of revolution.[2] As she argues, yearning after the coherent totality of an unbroken past is itself symptomatic of Modernity's own fragmentation. This is expressed, in turn, by the elevation of the fragment to a position of prominence as an aesthetic form, from poetry and philosophical writing to painting and sculpture. What wax suggests is the destruction of an absolute ideal or reality. The re-assembled body is contingent, both materially and imaginatively. Reassembly is speculative and uncertain,

1. Marjorie Hope Nicolson (1959) *Mountain Gloom and Mountain Glory: The De elopment of the Aesthetics of the Infinite*, University of Washington Press, Weyerhaeuser Environmental Classics-Reprint Edition, 1997.

2. Linda Nochlin, *The Body in Pieces: The Fragment as a Metaphor of Modernity*, Thames & Hudson, London and New York, 1994.

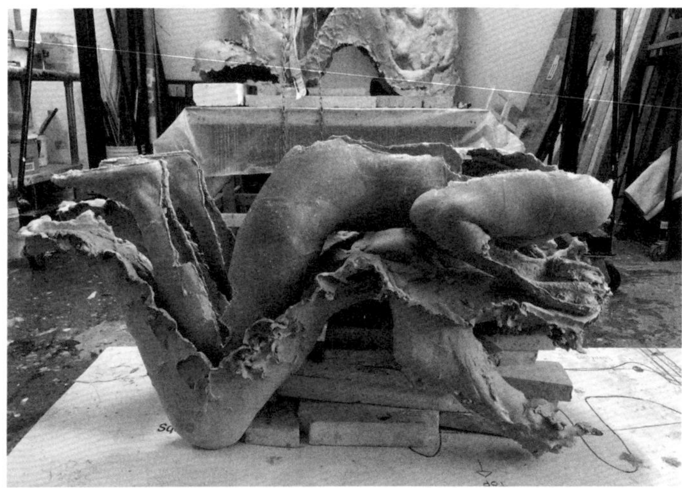

Fig. 2
Work in progress:
Calcify, 2019.
Brooklyn studio.

Fig. 3
Astronaut Sharon
Christa McAuliffe in
zero-G training aboard
NASA's zero gravity
aircraft. Photo by NASA/
Keith Meyers of the New
York Times.

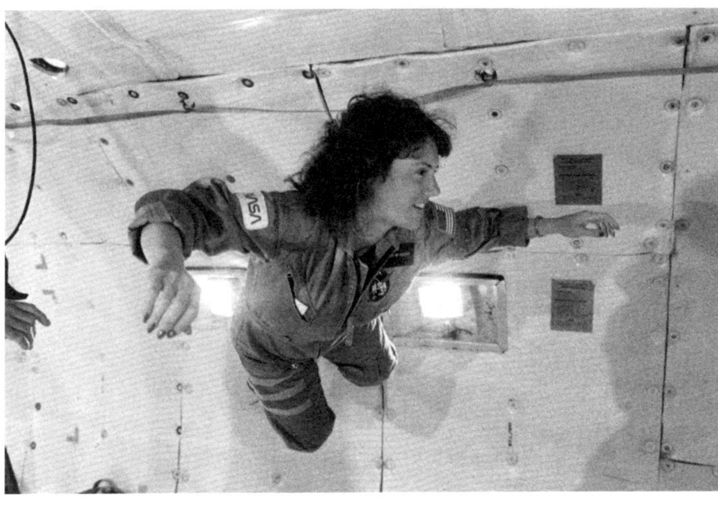

but it is also potentially more radical, as you also have the possibility of making things (people, worlds) differently.

NS__ You can melt wax down and reform it into a new face. You can grind plaster down to dust and reset it. Once the reliquary practice of casting from dead bodies and filling the subsequent mold is on the table, full-body mummification is not far away—closing the circle between relic and sculpture entirely. Ergo, Lenin: pumped full of chemicals—his corpse having become a mold for liquids, polymers, and waxes that take on his form from the inside. But I digress—The conceit of *Orogenesis* is the seeming reoccurrence of a particular body position (rounded back, arms held up in front) across different contexts: the pugilistic attitude of the *calchi*; Martha Graham's signature move, 'the contraction'; and what NASA has identified as the Neutral Body Posture assumed in zero gravity. But what is it that really *flows* throughout these contexts?

DH__ There is a certain essentialization of this pose that could only occur to a dancer or sculptor like Leite. A visceral intuition connects her investigations of Pompeii, dance, and space exploration. It is an association that might otherwise seem arbitrary. You can draw connections between Modern dance and the space age, as ideological gestures towards the future, for example. But the more significant issue is how the body, especially the female body, takes up space. These disparate contexts show us ways that the body can command or extend into space. It is not just a matter of appearance but, rather, the exhibition of the body's potentialities that is at stake.

The pugilistic attitude is an automatic posture assumed by a dead body as it is heated, causing the muscle tissue to contract. By contrast, Graham's contraction is a life pose: even as it purports to free the dancer from the deadening constraints of classical ballet and dusty ballroom choreographies, it requires a huge amount of energy and focus. It is expressive, in an ostensibly primitive sense, animalistic even—far from the passive, deathly pose of the *calchi*. It is, therefore, surprising that a zero-gravity context should produce the same posture. We might think of the body in outer-space as occupying a kind of liminal state between life and death, in which the astronaut loses muscle mass and is dependent upon an extensive technological prosthesis to survive, almost a state of suspended animation. Buried underground, dancing freely on the Earth's surface, or hovering above it, the body keeps on assuming this pose!

Is there some kind of corporeal wisdom at play in this position? Is it a pose we relax into? Or is it a mere compulsion? If so, what does it mean to take such a compulsion and transform it into an expressive practice, as per Graham's move, or Leite's sculptures? Assuming the pose deliberately, as Leite does in *Calcify*, offers a chance to interrogate what it feels like to be in this position unwillingly. The artist buries herself as if she was caught in the efflux of Vesuvius. Throughout the process she is conscious, whereas the historical victims were not. As such, there is a strange infusion of conscious awareness into the space of a dead body.

In contrast to an archaeological excavation, of symbols, artifacts, images or frescoes, Leite's method suggests an excavation of affect—of the experience of being present there as a body smothered under ash. Hers is an eerie supplement to the archaeologist's effort to reconstruct life as it was before the eruption. Perhaps through this reenactment there is a sense in which she seeks access to an afterlife lived *within* the space of the burial chamber, as imagined in the funerary practices of some cultures. In granting a measure of agency to the pugilistic attitude, the project gestures towards a transient state of being *before* the bodies disintegrated and left the empty spaces that would later be filled with plaster.

NS— Despite the formal evidence that Leite presents, it is not important for the viewer to truly believe that what looks similar *is* the same thing. By this I mean, whether one believes Martha Graham's claim that the 'contraction' is a key bodily expression (and/or whether the conceptual universe of this contraction necessarily maps onto the *calchi*) is *not* the the most interesting way into the project. Rather, it is enough to attend to the drama of Leite's *analogical thought*. Analogy is a pillar of the mythic imaginary—wherein 'if any entities or phenomena bear some resemblance, in any aspect, [then] they must be related'.[3] Under this rule, the imagination wanders and, all of a sudden, you imagine the *calchi* as dancers. It is a dark yet intriguing idea, these bodies dancing underground— beneath a cloud of ash, within the great scenographic extravaganza of a volcano destroying a Roman seaside town. It is the aestheticization of these figures; the basis of a thought that turns the *calchi*, dug up next to antique sculptures, into art too.

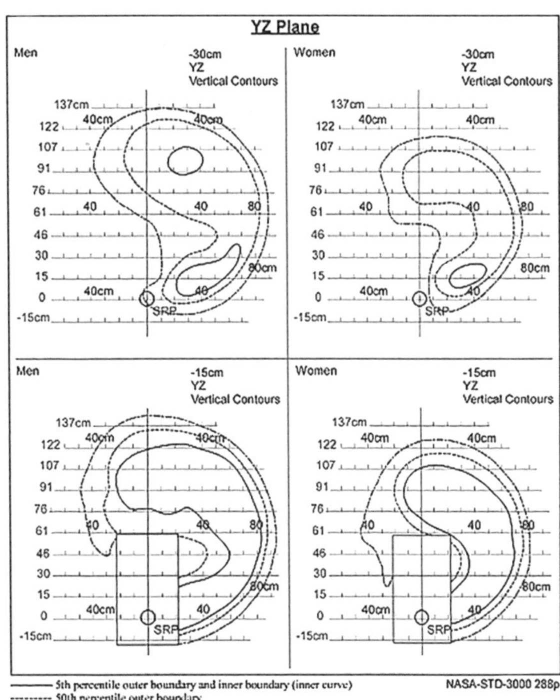

*Fig. 4
Grasp Reach Limits
with Right Hand for
American Male and
Female Populations*

Why not? They have already been displayed in various contexts, including museums. Leite's work demonstratively delivers them up to aesthetic judgment and delectation. It is almost *too much*, and that is where things get interesting: The gesture seems to uncover something latent. Moreover, while making the calchi (or the persons they were) dancers, the work also reframes the NASA special study of the human form as a question of creative representation. I should say, species self-representation: *Anthropometry* explores what representation of the human figure enables. How, for instance, does it extend the body's action in space? It would seem that rendering the human form effectively, in a systematic way, allows the body to act on a gigantic scale—exceeding the reach of the human hand, beyond a bio-corporeal scale, out towards the stars. Representation appears to be the original prosthesis. The image of the body and what it can do actually changes what the body really does—it enables it to do more.

DH— Leite builds *Anthropometry* by performing the possible range of arm reach motions from a seated position in a replica of a NASA space shuttle chair. This is the only work in the exhibition created with the

3. Elizabether Wayland Barber & Paul T. Barber, *When They Se ered Earth from Sky: How the Human Mind Shapes Myth*, Princeton University Press, New Jersey, 2004, p.34.

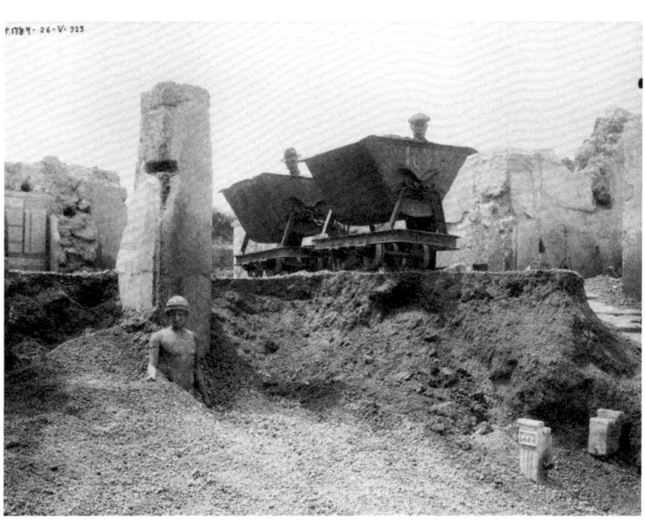

Fig. 5
Workers during
excavation of Pompeii,
date unknown c.1900.
Archaeological Park of
Pompeii, Photographic
Archive.

artist's distinctive procedure of carving out a void from within a block of wet clay and then casting it in plaster. Like the *calchi*, it is a cast of a space once occupied by a body in a liminal state. In this case, not a dead body but one dependent on an elaborate life support system, including the extensive energy, communications, and other technological infrastructure that makes space travel possible. We can think of this work as creating a fragment of hollow space that evokes the life that could be lived within it. Instead of a fragment of a larger solid form, Leite has offered us *Vestibule* (2017), *A Potential Space* (2016)—so many fractions of that limitless domain of (outer) space. Like fragments, these hollow spaces gesture at alternative spatial logics of completion.

NS__ I am reminded of the first chapter of Michel Serres' book *Statues*, which offers an astonishing triangulation in relation to what we are discussing. He comments on the Challenger rocket disaster of 1986, in which seven crew members were incinerated. He describes witnessing the event on television, and draws a parallel to ancient worship of the god Baal. Specifically, he talks about the Carthaginian practice of putting people inside a sculpture and burning it as a sacrifice to this deity. He writes that, in both cases, living bodies were interred within a casket of some kind and destroyed in front of a mass audience, and that the difference between the conceptual designation *idol/ sculpture* and *vehicle* is what separates the Challenger disaster from a sacrificial rite. The latter concept renders the explosion (and so many more mundane incidents, like car crashes) an 'accident' rather than an indicator of

structural depravity. Serres reminds us that the semantic difference *is* culture making. With the Challenger 'what stands, in the end, before the multitude is a Trojan horse leaving at a gallop for the moon'. Moreover, he concludes, 'the idol and the rocket are tombs'.[4] His ultimate question is 'are our scientific societies still founded on human sacrifice?' How does this bear on Pompeii? We have called the city's destruction an accident, but what if some part of its reality is something else? Certainly, interpreting the Pompeii disaster is a key rite for archaeologists focusing on the classical period. Leite is getting at something here…

DH__ Pompeii is a paradigmatic natural disaster. The site, frozen in time, appears to be set of a living theatre— replete with figures caught in the moment. It is *tragic* in the high poetic sense. In terms of its cultural genesis, tragedy converts the spectacle of human sacrifice into art, staging coming to terms with a terrible destiny and extracting a higher meaning therefrom. Pompeii is commonly allegorized as a natural disaster in which everyone is a hero because death is inevitable. Everyone, even the bit players in the narrative of Roman society, are remembered, in the form of the calchi. Even the servant girl is memorialized and, in a way, elevated to the status of the sculptures of gods and heroes buried beside her. Whereas the modern era wants for truly natural disasters (in which we are not, somehow, complicit), there is only glory in dying under the dramatic force of the volcano's fury.

NS__ You're right. That (myth-making) analogical regard puts the *calchi* and the classical statues on the same plane. It is an ecumenical thought, *from the present*. The tragedy happened in a classical historical moment, but the mythos of the *calchi* as heroes is part of our rite. The Romans made no statues with that kind of pathos. The Romantic take on Pompeii is that the the gods were buried with their people. A contemporary view would be that the people were elevated to the level of the gods.

4. Michel Serres, *Statues*, p.4.

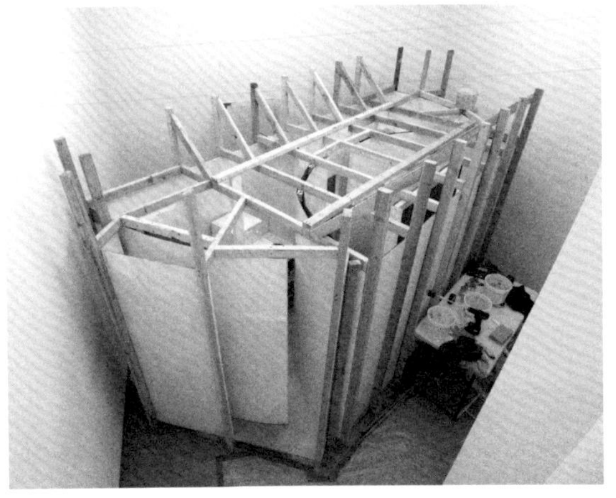

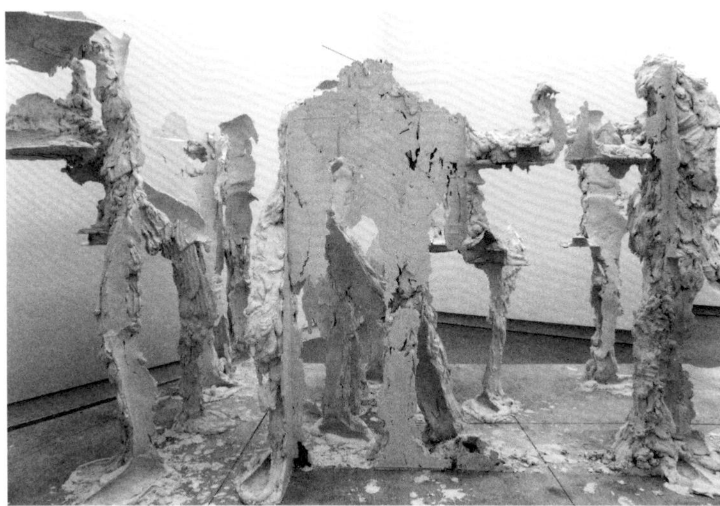

DH__   This is interesting because in the early 1990s an Icelandic vulcanologist named Haraldur Sigurdsson went to Indonesia's Mt Tambora, looking for the Pompeii of the East—a fantasy of a kingdom encapsulated intact under ash.[5] It is not so much that a fabulous well-developed society/settlement was reputed to have existed there, but more that the prospect of being buried under a volcano confers grandeur. He did find some things on his first excavation, but further digging yielded little else. There is a metaphorical traffic between the way in which a society falls and the value that it appears to have.

NS__   Let's talk about the rite. Contemporary life is, arguably, an ongoing disaster. Moreover, following Serres, it appears as though our society *is* founded on human sacrifice. Now, when Leite draws a line between the *calchi* and Martha Graham's work it is hard not to view the 'contraction' as a flinch. The circulation of implication (in *Orogenesis*), which makes the *calchi* dancers, also sets up Graham's modern dancers as performing some kind of trauma: It makes the contraction a death dance; a spasmodic beat in a death rattle.

DH__   The other way to think about *Anthropometry* is that it is exactly how you would try to dig yourself out of your own grave. Instead of an exuberant dancer, the astronaut becomes a flaccid little worm, groping around inside a tin can. It is morbid….

NS__   And we should mention that Leite's last

important project was an engagement with Amazonian funeral urns of a spherical shape.

DH__   There is something very important about Leite's invitation to imagine your own embodiment by seeing an image of the space that you take up; literally, the volume traced out by postures and gestures. Here is a woman performing the act of taking up space and monumentalizing that performance. NASA had to cancel what would have been the first all female spacewalk, recently, because they only had one space suit in a woman's size. The mission was eagerly anticipated for its symbolic significance. That old saying "you make the path by walking" stings when a way forward is obstructed. Making space for oneself is an intensely laborious process. Leite exhibits this, by digging, groping, and scooping her way through immense mounds of clay.

In *Anthropometry*, she is exploring a pose in which everything one needs is within arms' reach. It is a pose in which all of the conditions of life are designed to be as manageable as possible for a worker operating within a very small space. In *SHEE* (2018) Leite investigated another architectural prosthesis of the space program, the Self-Deployable Habitat for Extreme Environments (SHEE)—a robotic expandable structure meant to facilitate simulations of life on Mars, and offer shelter in disaster zones and terrestrial extremes. Rather than casting the nominally comfortable living environs offered by this protected bubble, Leite excavated the interstices of the apparatus in its collapsed form. She was interested in what is prior to open space, and all the support

5. Site of the largest volcanic eruption in the last 10,000 years (1815).

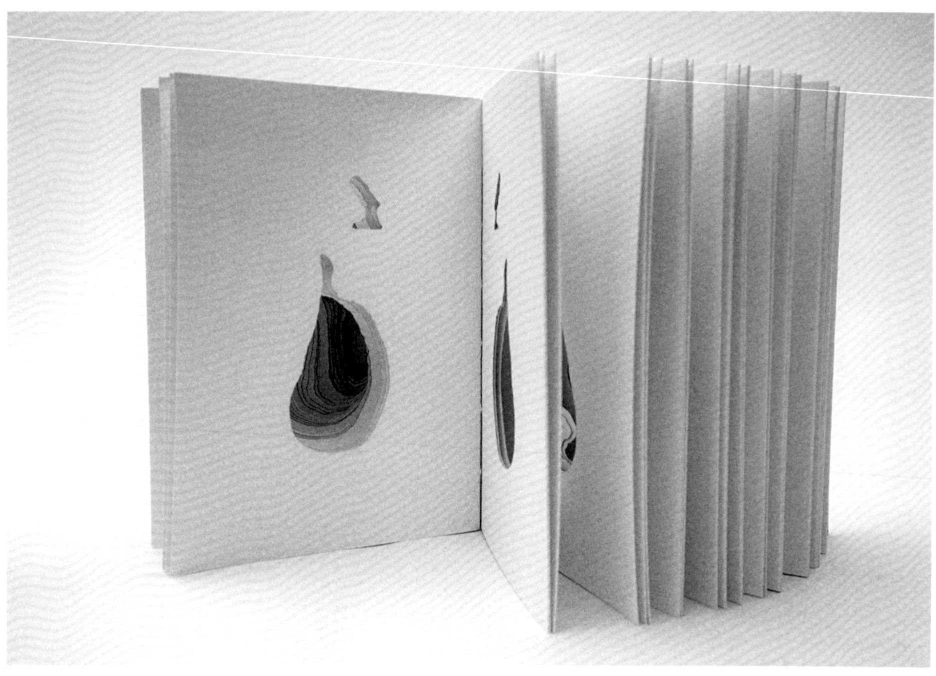

infrastructure involved in keeping it open, so she crawled around in the collapsed structure, taking its measure with her body and plaster.

Is there an impulse to life in the space program, or is it a death wish—the nihilism of a culture that projects its fantasy of life into space while neglecting the habitability of our own planet? Where does taking up space with a life impulse begin, with respect to outer space? Does it begin with a female body? Personally, I think the contemporary outer space program is death-wish bullshit. But Juliana is performing what it means for a female body to take up space within the apparatus of the space program. Hers is a different agenda, to press the analogy all the way, in Leite's sculptural logic she is looking for the vagina of the space program. She treats SHEE the same way she treats the vagina in *A Potential Space*, which is created by making a mold of the vagina using alginate, a soft body-casting material. In a philosophical sense, this project employed a particular method of body casting to look at what the vagina is *in and for itself* rather than *for another*—a penis, or the phallus.

NS__ I like that. Her artistic agenda *is* the Female Space Program. This wordplay lets us speak about a female relation to a state techno-industrial project that colonizes outer space (usually on behalf of men). But it also lets us address the exploration of spatial agency at the level of individual (female) bodies—what can be reached, etc. In this latter sense, perhaps the Male Space Program was traditional fine art. This double implication

also illuminates the distinction between accident and rite. What is rite delivers *rights*. The accident of one's body as female, for instance, is set against the choreography of a galactic phallus; the erection a prosthesis that pushes outward towards the stars. A massive tool.

It seems as though the female space program cannot operate in virgin space, because the idea of such space underpins the male space program. The female space program has to trace its own path *through* cosmic manspreading; it has to dig its way, find a potential space *within* this big other; within a manspreading that reaches from the grave to the stars. I think that this is what you mean by finding the vagina of the space program. And I suppose that this new path (or program) traverses regions that the male space program has trodden, and finds them littered with statues, heroes, and limbs. It works its way through a ground of male images, or figural manifestations of a male space—sculptures of dicks; sculptures made *by* dicks—and uncovers a potential space for (another) sculpture, in places unrecognized as such, wherein things like the *calchi* are revalued.

DH__ Right—how do we explore space without merely projecting into it whatever assumptions, desires, or investments will fit? This is precisely the point in Leite's previous work *A Potential Space*. How do you find out what shape a vagina is, other than having it assume the shape of a speculum, a dildo, a dick? It resists being known. It remains a hiding place (a place that hides).

There is an art to palpating space(s)—as there is to knowing the past. In fact, one could compare the eighteenth century desire to possess antiquity to the space race today.

NS__   *Orogenesis* takes place amid the recovered objects from the Villa dei Papyri: an upper-class domestic collection that includes busts of philosophers, poets, etc. So, Leite's sculptures are installed within a pantheon of historical and allegorical figures. While her motif is, in one sense, formal (some sculptures come into being through algorithmic processes, based on repetitions and rules), an invitation to myth and allegory obtains. That after digging through the layers, visitors should uncover a female space program, an inner space, demonstrates that Leite's project is in no way classicizing. Sometimes the most contemporary artistic statements actually take place in a museum full of old marble. In as much as we might marvel at the balanced and polished forms of the Villa dei Papyri sculptures, and observe them pulsing with Olympian divinity, Leite's repetition and fragmentation monumentalizes the body anew. Leite speaks to the body's fleeting temporality—a being that is only partially visible during any given action. Her work suggests a finite body in an unfinished representation. This aesthetic conjures more of that particular body; more body to come; more embodiment. *Orogenesis* is not solely an activation of the national museum's collection, as much as a fundamental statement about occupying space…

DH__   Yes, but finally, I want to return to moving mountains, to orogenesis. There is also an insight about our relationship to force; natural forces, technological might, the agency of our own body here. Leite's *Orogenesis* is a dance of receptivity to forces that overwhelm us. The weight of matter and history on our bodies. Playing with the question of how we position ourselves in relation to threats, it demonstrates the importance of resistance to maintaining muscle mass, literally and figuratively. The distinction between mountains and volcanoes is that the volcano always holds the potential for change from within, as opposed to the mountain, which erodes from without. There is something suggestive about the volcano for Leite's practice, in so far it is odd, as a sculptor, to dig her way through out of a mass of matter, rather than chiseling away at it from the outside. Leite's sculptural practice operates within the subduction zone, in sculpture's unstable ground, where there is always potential for new becoming.

Mario Codognato__

is a curator, who was since its foundation in 2005 the chief curator of MADRE, Naples. He also curated contemporary art exhibitions at the Archeological Museum in Naples, including Francesco Clemente (2002), Jeff Koons (2003), Anish Kapoor (2003), Richard Serra (2004), Anselm Kiefer (2004) and the first ever museum retrospective of Damien Hirst (2004). From 2014 to 2016 he was chief curator at the 21er Haus of the Belvedere in Vienna.

Dehlia Hannah__

is a philosopher and curator, currently Mads Øvlisen Postdoctoral Fellow at the Department of Chemistry and Biosciences at Aalborg University-Copenhagen; an affiliate of the Laboratory for Past Disaster Science at Aarhus University; and the School of Earth and Space Exploration at Arizona State University. She holds a Ph.D. in Philosophy from Columbia University, with specializations in philosophy of science and aesthetics.

Nadim Samman__

is a curator and art historian. He read Philosophy at University College London before receiving his PhD from the Courtauld Institute of Art. He co-founded the 1st Antarctic Biennale (2017) and the Antarctic Pavilion (Venice, 2015-). In 2016 he curated the 5th Moscow International Biennale for Young Art, and in 2012 the 4th Marrakech Biennale (with Carson Chan).

Dehlia Hannah e Nadim Samman

DH__ Quando le placche tettoniche si scontrano, la pressione laterale può causare due situazioni: o lo strato superficiale viene spinto verso l'alto lungo entrambi i lati della linea di faglia, formando catene montuose, oppure una delle placche si inserisce sotto l'altra, dando origine ai vulcani. Questo processo è chiamato orogenesi. Terremoti e montagne ardenti hanno sempre catturato l'immaginazione collettiva, hanno un ruolo di primo piano nei miti delle origini, sono metafora di agitazioni politiche e turbamenti psicologici. Il Vesuvio è il caso paradigmatico di un vulcano che ha distrutto, e tuttavia preservato, un mondo. Forse, dal punto di vista del suo significato culturale, è stato persino creativo. Nella sua pratica di scultrice, la Leite spesso conferisce una forma solida a gesti e movimenti dinamici, come l'azione di arrampicarsi o raggiungere qualcosa. Evocando la nascita delle montagne, il titolo di questa mostra propone analogie tra le configurazioni geologiche della materia e le posizioni che il corpo umano assume.

NS__ In molti dei suoi lavori, la Leite realizza nudi femminili in gesso. La scelta di questo medium coinvolge particolari tropi simbolici e artistici: il gesso è un materiale neoclassico, ed entriamo pertanto immediatamente nell'ambito discorsivo che concerne la maniera in cui un corpo dovrebbe essere rappresentato. Per le Belle Arti, le sculture classiche come quelle conservate nel Museo Archeologico Nazionale erano gli esempi migliori. Manufatti come i marmi farnesi e quelli ospitati alla Villa dei Papiri erano lezioni fatte oggetto. In molte accademie, i calchi in gesso di tali sculture venivano usati come modelli a cui ispirarsi. Aspirando a stabilire una relazione individuale con i maggiori trionfi dell'arte classica (sia sul piano artistico che anche, forse, su quello della soggettività) gli accademici cercavano di fissare (piuttosto letteralmente in effetti) uno standard basato sull'eccellenza, attraverso una profusione di copie di gesso. Con l'impiego di questo materiale indicizzato, il gesso, un determinato aspetto dell'arte accademica diventava dunque un tributo all'antica scultura monumentale e ai suoi corpi. Ma come avrebbe mai potuto riuscire nel suo intento?

Ad esempio, prendiamo in considerazione i famosi calchi. Corpi umani sepolti sotto la cenere di Pompei esistiti giusto il tempo di permettere la creazione di stampi in negativo, a partire da una catastrofe naturale. Successivamente, questi calchi sono stati riempiti dall'azione dell'uomo. I calchi sono infatti getti di gesso positivi dello spazio negativo lasciato dai corpi. Il progetto della Leite invita ora a speculare sulla funzione politica dei calchi come un tipo di sculture monumentali (o sculture-reliquie). Assecondando questa riflessione, dobbiamo domandarci se sono meri monumenti alla vita idiosincratica di determinate persone, e della tragedia che ha colpito la città di Pompei, o se operano in un'altra direzione. Nel contesto di questa mostra, potrebbero, ad esempio, sostenere un qualche tipo di proposizione spirituale o metafisica in relazione alle figure scultoree recuperate dallo stesso sito? Si può guardare allora alle sculture di Juliana come mediatori concettuali tra i calchi e le sculture classiche della Villa dei Papiri. Sembra però che riguardino anche qualcosa di più di questo...

DH__ È interessante considerare come questo antico mondo sia stato rievocato per servire

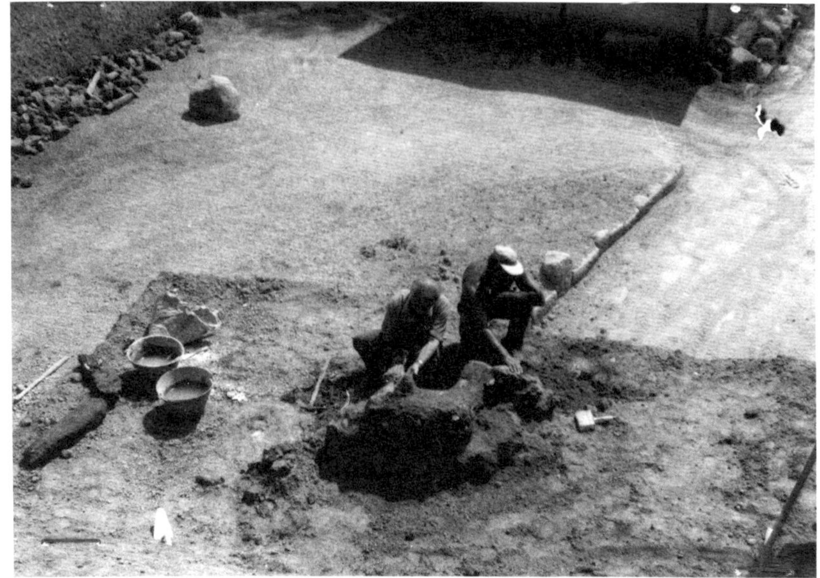

l'immaginazione moderna. Gli scavi di Pompei iniziarono a metà del XVIII secolo, alimentando un'ossessione per l'antichità (e per le antichità) che attirò viaggiatori d'élite nel Grand Tour attraverso le Alpi, fino a Roma, e poi più a sud, fino a Napoli. Con questo tipo di viaggio nacquero nuove categorie estetiche. Una volta considerate ostacoli brutti e pericolosi sulla rotta verso le bellezze dell'Italia, le montagne divennero sublimi[1]. Le statue rotte divennero veicolo di immaginazione per i Romantici. Tra le rovine, poeti e filosofi trovarono la chiave per la grandezza di un passato perduto, simboli di lutto per la caduta terrena della Modernità da un antico stato di grazia. Dal pezzo di una scultura classica rotta (una mano, un piede) si potrebbe estrapolare la figura completa. Questa operazione di sforzo immaginativo si affida alla logica implicita di un corpo idealizzato, la cui perfetta rappresentazione scultorea è suggerita da qualsiasi elemento. In definitiva, il frammento diventa forma estetica a sé stante, e le opere d'arte e la letteratura vengono create "non finite".

Come tu hai giustamente osservato, il progetto della Leite fa dialogare la reliquia con la scultura classica per mezzo del manufatto documentario tratto dagli scavi archeologici. Se i frammenti sono veicoli per l'immaginazione, le reliquie sono veicoli per l'anima: un capello, un'unghia, un brandello di indumento, un osso del piede di un santo, sono capaci di ancorare una presenza spirituale al tempo storico. Interagendo con i calchi in quanto forme estetiche, la Leite li offre

contemporaneamente anche come indici di corpi profani. Quindi, così come le reliquie religiose, anche i calchi contengono frammenti di una vita, anche se di una vita quotidiana. Il frammento di una scultura classica non è solo il pezzo di una figura che è bella nelle sue proporzioni formali. Essa offre uno sguardo su un mondo di vita in cui gli dèi erano presenti ed erano portati in modo sostanziale all'interno di tali artefatti. La Leite ritorna a Pompei per scavare altre logiche estetiche usando nuove pratiche corporee e materiali.

NS— Rimanendo sui materiali e sul loro significato: il nesso tra gesso e reliquia è la maschera mortuaria. Nello stato "illuminato" della Francia del XVIII secolo, la religiosità arcaica e il moderno confluirono in questa pratica quasi scultorea. Ricordiamo infatti come la prima attività di Madame Tussaud fu produrre calchi delle teste mozzate che cadevano dalla ghigliottina. Alcuni eroi (ordinati dal non completamente antico regime della monarchia cristiana) dovettero essere deposti, prima che il Neoclassicismo post-rivoluzionario potesse prendere piede nelle arti, e prima che il reliquiario colmasse il vuoto tra l'arte di per sé e il mondo come un progetto estetico. Dopo aver abbattuto le vecchie statue, e frammentato molti corpi reali, i calchi in gesso di facce emersero come sintomi chiave di un corpo post-rivoluzionario. Detto questo, dovremmo notare che questi quasi-monumenti positivi, presi da calchi negativi, sono fatti di cera, qualcosa di ancora più molle e fragile del gesso, che si avvicina più al liquido. Certamente, questa è una metafora suggestiva per la politica moderna: la realtà è infinitamente malleabile. Scolpibile.

1. Marjorie Hope Nicolson (1959) *Mountain Gloom and Mountain Glory: The De elopment of the Aesthetics of the Infinite*, University of Washington Press, Weyerhaeuser Environmental Classics-Reprint Edition, 1997.

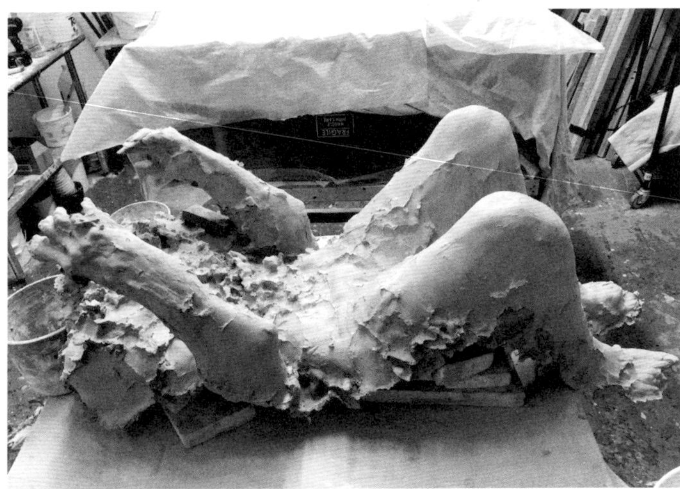

Fig. 2
Calcify in fase di realizzazione, 2019. Studio di Brooklyn

Fig. 3
Controlli sulla tuta russa Sokol dell'astronauta Edward T. Lu, The Soyuz Integration Facility presso Baikonur Cosmodrome in Baikonur, Kazakhstan, 2003. Foto di NASA/Bill Ingalls.

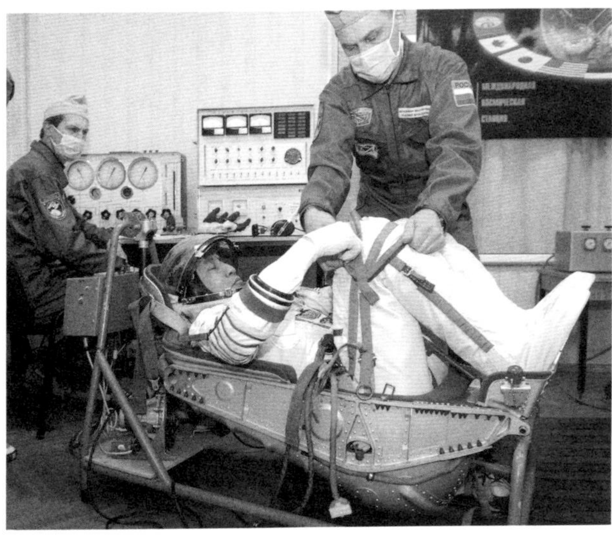

radicale, in quanto si ha anche la possibilità di rendere le cose (persone, mondi) in modo diverso.

NS__ Puoi sciogliere la cera e ridarle forma in una nuova faccia. Puoi sbriciolare il gesso e rifarlo. E una volta che la pratica reliquiaria di fare calchi di cadaveri e riempirne lo stampo è sdoganata, non siamo molto lontani dalla mummificazione, completando così il percorso che collega reliquia e scultura. Ergo, Lenin: pompato di sostanze chimiche, il suo cadavere è diventato uno stampo per liquidi, polimeri e cere che assumono la sua forma dall'interno. Ma sto divagando…

Il concetto che sta alla base del progetto Orogenesi è l'apparente ripetersi di una particolare posizione del corpo (schiena ricurva, braccia alzate sul davanti) in diversi contesti: la postura da pugile dei calchi di Pompei, la mossa caratteristica di Martha Graham ("la contrazione") e ciò che la NASA ha identificato come "la postura neutra" che il corpo assume a gravità zero. Ma cosa attraversa davvero tutti questi contesti?

D__ C'è una sorta di sublimazione di questa posa, che potrebbe accadere solo a un ballerino o a uno scultore come la Leite. Un'intuizione viscerale collega le sue ricerche su Pompei, la danza e l'esplorazione dello spazio. È un parallelo che potrebbe altrimenti sembrare arbitrario. Puoi tracciare connessioni tra la danza moderna e l'era spaziale, in quanto gesti ideologici protesi verso il futuro, per esempio. Ma il problema più significativo è come il corpo, in particolare il corpo femminile, occupa lo spazio. Questi contesti disparati ci mostrano diversi modi in cui il corpo può dominare lo spazio, o espandersi in esso. Non è solo una questione di apparenza ma, piuttosto si tratta dell'esibizione delle potenzialità del corpo che è in gioco.

DH__ Mi viene in mente l'argomentazione di Linda Nochlin secondo cui, dopo l'uso iconico della ghigliottina durante la Rivoluzione Francese, il frammento è sempre accompagnato dalla promessa (e dalla minaccia) della rivoluzione[2]. Come lei sostiene, anelare alla totalità di un passato coerente e unitario è di per sé sintomatico della frammentazione propria della Modernità stessa. Ciò è espresso, a sua volta, dall'elevazione del frammento a una posizione di rilievo come forma estetica, nella poesia e nella scrittura filosofica così come nella pittura e nella scultura. Ciò che la cera suggerisce è la distruzione di un ideale assoluto, o la distruzione della realtà. Il corpo ri-assemblato è quindi contingente, sia a livello materiale che immaginativo. L'azione del ricostruire è speculativa e incerta, ma è anche potenzialmente più

2. Linda Nochlin, *The Body in Pieces: The Fragment as a Metaphor of Modernity*, Thames & Hudson, London and New York, 1994.

La postura da pugile è la posizione automatica assunta da un cadavere quando viene sottoposto al calore, a causa della contrazione del tessuto muscolare. Al contrario, la contrazione della Graham è una posa vitale: anche se intende liberare il danzatore dai limiti massacranti del balletto classico e delle coreografie delle polverose sale da ballo, questo richiede un'enorme quantità di energia e concentrazione. È espressiva, in un senso ostentatamente primitivo, addirittura animale - lontano dalla posa passiva, mortale dei calchi. È pertanto sorprendente che un contesto a gravità zero possa causare la stessa postura. Potremmo pensare al corpo nello spazio come entità che occupa una sorta di stato liminale tra la vita e la morte, in cui l'astronauta perde la massa muscolare e dipende da un'ampia protesi tecnologica per sopravvivere, trovandosi quasi in uno stato di animazione sospesa. Seppellito nel sottosuolo, danzando liberamente sulla superficie terrestre o librandosi sopra di essa, il corpo continua ad assumere questa posa!

C'è in gioco un qualche tipo di saggezza corporea, in questa posizione? È una posa in cui ci rilassiamo? O è una semplice pulsione? Se è così, che cosa significa prendere una tale compulsione e trasformarla in una pratica espressiva, come per la mossa della Graham, o le sculture della Leite? Assumere questa posa deliberatamente, come la Leite fa in *Calcify*, offre la possibilità di interrogarsi sul come ci si senta a stare in questa posizione controvoglia. L'artista si seppellisce come se fosse stata raggiunta dall'eruzione del Vesuvio. Durante tutto il processo è cosciente, mentre le vittime storiche non lo erano. Come tale, c'è quindi una strana infusione di consapevolezza cosciente dentro lo spazio di un corpo morto.

A differenza di uno scavo archeologico (di simboli, artefatti, immagini o affreschi) il metodo della Leite suggerisce uno scavo di affetto - dell'esperienza dell'essere presenti lì, come un corpo soffocato sotto la cenere. La sua è un'inquietante integrazione al lavoro che l'archeologo fa per risalire a com'era la vita prima dell'eruzione.

Forse in questa rievocazione c'è un senso, in cui lei cerca un accesso a un aldilà vissuto dentro lo spazio della camera funeraria, come immaginato nelle pratiche funerarie di alcune culture. Nel conferire alla postura da pugile una certa dose di autorità, il progetto mira a uno stato d'essere transitorio, prima che i corpi si disintegrino e lascino spazi vuoti, che verranno poi riempiti dal gesso.

NS__	Nonostante l'evidenza formale che la Leite presenta, per lo spettatore non è fondamentale credere che gli elementi simili siano effettivamente la stessa cosa. Con questo intendo che credere o

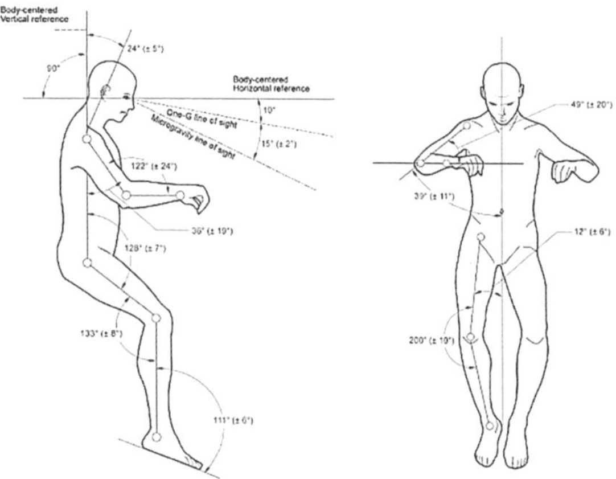

Fig. 4
Posizione Neutrale del Corpo a gravità zero, definita dal Manned Systems Integration Standards Handbook della NASA, 1995

meno all'affermazione di Martha Graham che la "contrazione" sia un'espressione chiave del corpo (o se l'universo concettuale di questa contrazione sia necessariamente riconducibile ai calchi) non è la lettura più interessante per questo progetto. Piuttosto, è sufficiente assistere al dramma che l'analogia della Leite presenta. L'analogia è un pilastro dell'immaginario mitico, in cui "se delle entità, o fenomeni, riportano qualche somiglianza, in qualsiasi aspetto, [allora] essi devono essere correlati"[3]. Stando a questa regola, l'immaginazione vaga e, all'improvviso, ti trovi a pensare ai calchi come a dei danzatori. È un'idea oscura, ma intrigante: questi corpi che danzano sottoterra, sotto una nuvola di cenere, nella spettacolare scenografia di un vulcano che distrugge una città romana. L'estetizzazione di queste figure è il fondamento di un pensiero che trasforma anche i calchi, scavati accanto a sculture antiche, in arte.

Perché no? Sono già stati esposti in vari contesti, musei inclusi. Il lavoro della Leite li espone ora deliberatamente al giudizio e alla fruizione estetica. È quasi troppo, ed è qui che le cose si fanno interessanti: il gesto sembra svelare qualcosa di latente. Inoltre, nel trasformare i calchi (o le persone che erano) in danzatori, l'opera riformula anche lo speciale studio della NASA sulla forma umana come una questione di rappresentazione creativa. Dovrei dire, una specie di auto-rappresentazione: *Antropometria* esplora ciò che la raffigurazione della figura umana consente. Come, ad esempio, contribuisce a far estendere l'azione del corpo nello spazio? Sembrerebbe che riprodurre la forma umana in modo efficace, in modo sistematico, consenta al corpo di agire su una scala gigantesca, superando la portata della mano umana, al di là di una dimensione bio-corporea, fuori, verso le stelle. La rappresentazione sembra essere la protesi originale. L'immagine del corpo e di ciò che può

3. Elizabether Wayland Barber & Paul T. Barber, *When They Severed Earth from Sky: How the Human Mind Shapes Myth*, Princeton University Press, New Jersey, 2004, p.34.

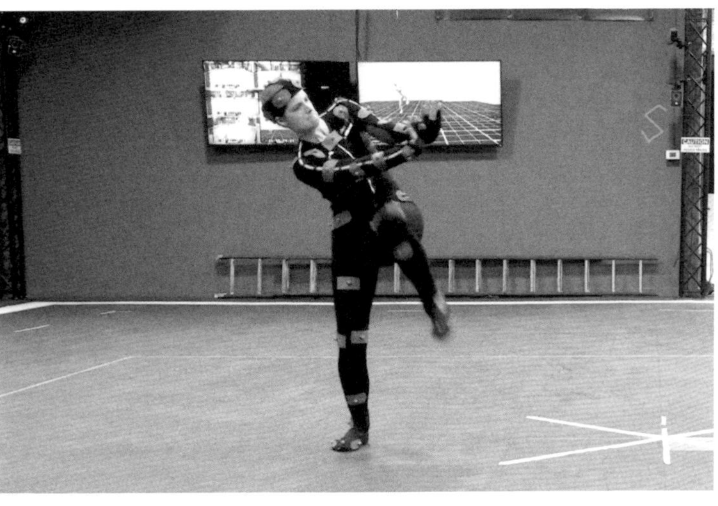

fare effettivamente cambia ciò che il corpo fa davvero: gli consente di fare di più.

DH__ La Leite costruisce *Antropometria* eseguendo tutta la possibile gamma di movimenti di estensione del braccio stando seduta su una replica di un sedile di uno shuttle della NASA. Questa è l'unica opera della mostra creata con il tipico procedimento dell'artista di scavare un vuoto dall'interno di un blocco di argilla umida, per poi farne un calco in gesso. Come i calchi di Pompei, è il calco di uno spazio precedentemente occupato da un corpo in uno stato liminale. In questo caso, non un corpo morto, ma uno dipendente da un elaborato sistema di supporto vitale, compresa l'energia, le comunicazioni e altre infrastrutture tecnologiche che rendono possibile il viaggio nello spazio. Possiamo allora pensare a questo lavoro come alla creazione di un frammento di spazio vuoto che richiama la vita che potrebbe essere stata vissuta al suo interno. Invece di un frammento di una forma solida più grande, la Leite ci ha offerto *Vestibule* (2017) e *A Potential Space* (2016), tante frazioni di quel dominio infinito che è lo spazio. Come i frammenti, questi spazi vuoti mirano a logiche spaziali di completamento alternative.

NS__ Mi viene in mente il primo capitolo del libro di Michel Serres "Statues", che offre una sorprendente triangolazione in relazione a quello di cui stiamo parlando. L'autore del libro commenta il disastro del missile Challenger nel 1986, in cui sette membri dell'equipaggio furono inceneriti. Descrive di aver assistito all'evento in televisione e traccia un parallelo con l'antico culto del dio Baal. Nello specifico, parla della pratica cartaginese di mettere le persone

dentro una scultura e bruciarla come sacrificio per questa divinità. Scrive che, in entrambi i casi, corpi viventi vengono sepolti in un qualche tipo di feretro e distrutti di fronte a un pubblico, e che la differenza tra la definizione concettuale di idolo/scultura e quella di veicolo è ciò che separa il disastro di Challenger da un rito sacrificale. Quest'ultimo concetto rende l'esplosione (e molti altri eventi terreni, come gli incidenti automobilistici) un "incidente", piuttosto che un indicatore di perversione strutturale. Serres ci ricorda che la differenza semantica è il creare cultura. Con il Challenger "alla fine, ciò che sta di fronte alla moltitudine è un cavallo di Troia che galoppa verso la luna". Inoltre, conclude, "l'idolo e il razzo sono tombe"[4]. La sua domanda, in definitiva, è: "le nostre società scientifiche sono ancora basate sul sacrificio umano?" E in che modo questo ci riconduce a Pompei? Abbiamo definito la distruzione della città "un incidente", ma se una parte della sua realtà fosse qualcos'altro? Certamente, interpretare il disastro di Pompei è un rito fondamentale per gli archeologi che si concentrano sul periodo classico. La Leite dunque qui sta arrivando a qualcosa....

DH__ Pompei è un disastro naturale paradigmatico. Il sito, congelato nel tempo, sembra essere un teatro vivente, pieno di figure colte nel momento. È tragico, nella più alta accezione poetica del termine. Sotto il profilo della sua genesi culturale, infatti, la tragedia trasforma lo spettacolo del sacrificio umano in arte, mettendo in scena uno scendere a patti con un terribile destino ed estrapolandone quindi un significato più alto. Pompei è comunemente allegorizzata come un disastro naturale in cui ognuno è un eroe, poiché la morte era inevitabile. Tutti, anche i più piccoli attori nella narrazione della società romana, sono ricordati, per mezzo dei calchi. Anche la serva è ricordata e, in un certo senso, elevata allo status delle sculture degli dei e degli eroi sepolti accanto a lei. Mentre l'era moderna manca di veri disastri naturali (di cui noi non siamo, in qualche modo, complici), qui c'è solo gloria, nel morire sotto la forza drammatica della furia del vulcano.

NS__ Hai ragione. Il piano dell'analogia (che genera il mito) mette i calchi e le statue classiche sullo stesso livello. È un pensiero ecumenico, dal presente. La tragedia è avvenuta in un momento storico classico, ma il mito dei calchi come eroi fa parte del nostro rito. I romani non creavano statue con quel tipo di pathos. La successiva interpretazione romantica di Pompei fu che gli dei furono sepolti con la loro gente. Una possibile versione contemporanea sarebbe che le persone vengono elevate al livello degli dei.

DH__ Questo è interessante, perché nei primi anni Novanta un vulcanologo islandese di nome Haraldur

4. Michel Serres, *Statues*, p.4.

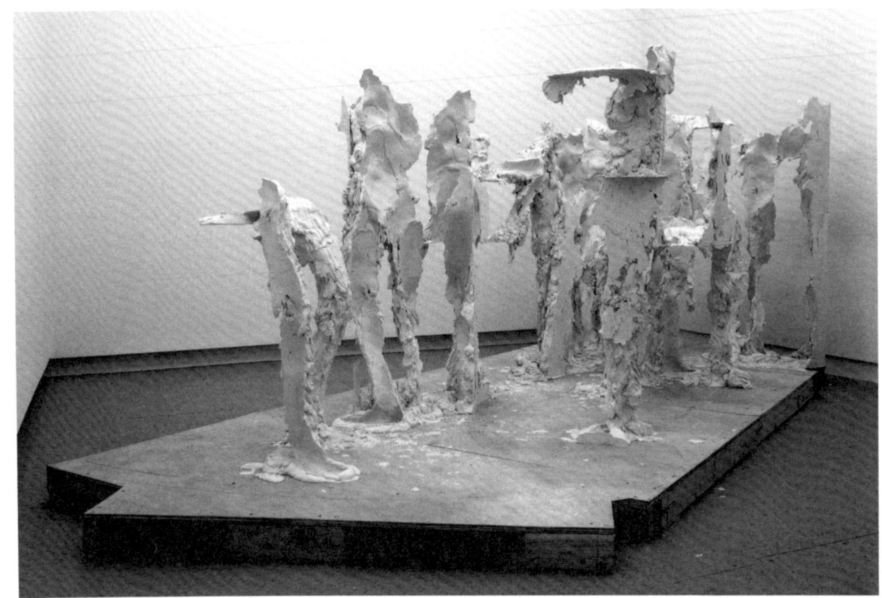

Sigurdsson si recò presso il monte Tambora, in Indonesia, alla ricerca della Pompei dell'est - la fantasia di un regno incapsulato intatto sotto la cenere[5]. Ciò che incuriosiva era non tanto il fatto che si credesse che lì fosse esistita una società sorprendentemente sviluppata, quanto l'idea che fosse sepolta sotto un vulcano, cosa che conferisce un certo fascino. Effettivamente, il vulcanologo ha poi trovato alcune cose nel suo primo scavo, ma ulteriori scavi non hanno fornito molto di più. C'è un traffico metaforico tra il modo in cui una società cade e il valore che sembra avere.

NS__ Ma parliamo del rito. La vita contemporanea è, verosimilmente, un continuo disastro. Inoltre, stando a Serres, sembra che la nostra società sia fondata sul sacrificio umano. Ora, quando la Leite traccia una linea di divisione tra i calchi e il lavoro di Martha Graham, è difficile non vedere la "contrazione" come un'esitazione. Il fatto che esistano (in *Orogenesi*) delle implicazioni per le quali i calchi diventano danzatori, fa sì che anche i ballerini moderni della Graham possano essere interpretati come nell'atto di rappresentare una sorta di trauma: rende la contrazione una danza mortale, un battito spasmodico in un rantolo di morte.

DH__ L'altro modo di pensare ad *Antropometria* è che è esattamente il movimento di scavo che faresti per provare a uscire fuori dalla tua stessa tomba. Invece di un danzatore esuberante, l'astronauta diventa un piccolo verme flaccido che brancola dentro una scatola di latta. È quasi macabro...

NS__ A questo punto dovremmo anche ricordare che l'ultimo importante progetto della Leite riguardava le urne funerarie amazzoniche di forma sferica.

DH__ C'è qualcosa di molto importante nell'invito della Leite a immaginare la tua incarnazione vedendo un'immagine dello spazio. Letteralmente: il volume occupato da posture e gesti. E qui c'è una donna che compie l'atto di occupare lo spazio e monumentalizzare quella performance. Recentemente, la NASA ha dovuto cancellare quella che sarebbe stata la prima passeggiata spaziale tutta al femminile, perché avevano solo una tuta spaziale adatta a una donna. La missione era attesissima per il suo significato simbolico. Ecco che quel vecchio detto "il cammino si fa camminando" stride, quando il cammino da seguire è ostacolato. Guadagnarsi il proprio spazio è un processo faticoso. Ed è questo ciò che la Leite mostra, scavando, brancolando e aprendosi una strada attraverso immensi mucchi di argilla.

In *Antropometria*, l'autrice sta esplorando una posa in cui tutto ciò di cui si ha bisogno è a portata di mano. È una posa in cui tutte le condizioni per la vita sono progettate per essere il più possibile gestibili per una persona che opera in uno spazio molto piccolo. In *SHEE* (2018) la Leite aveva studiato un'altra protesi architettonica del programma spaziale, l'Habitat Autonomo per Ambienti Estremi (*SHEE*), una struttura robotica espandibile pensata per facilitare le simulazioni di vita su Marte e per offrire riparo in aree disastrate e ai confini del pianeta. Piuttosto che fare il calco di quei comodi ambienti offerti da questa bolla protetta, la Leite ha preferito scavare gli interstizi di quell'apparato nella sua forma crollata. L'artista era interessata a ciò che precede lo spazio, e a tutta l'infrastruttura di supporto necessaria per

Fig. 6
SHEE, 2018.
Particolare. 426 x
179 x 210cm. Scultura
site-specific. Hydrocal,
acciaio, pigmenti. Foto:
Greg Carideo, courtesy
Arsenal Contemporary

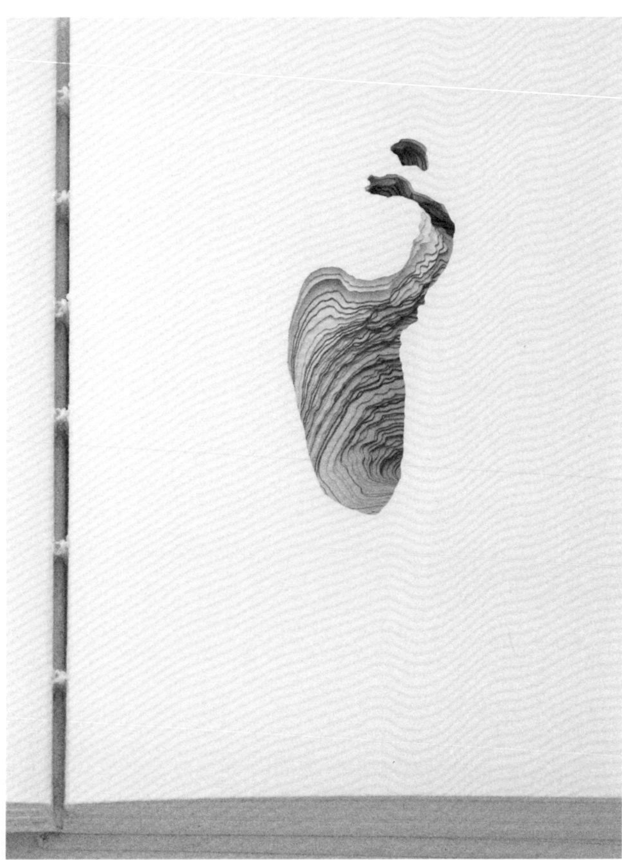

tenerlo aperto, così si è infilata nella struttura crollata, misurandola con il suo corpo e con il gesso.

C'è un impulso alla vita nel programma spaziale, o è un desiderio di morte, il nichilismo di una cultura che proietta le sue fantasie di vita nello spazio mentre trascura l'abitabilità del nostro pianeta? Dove ha inizio il desiderio di occupare lo spazio per assecondare un impulso vitale, in relazione allo spazio esterno? Ha inizio con il corpo femminile? Personalmente, penso che il programma spaziale contemporaneo sia uno stupido istinto di morte. Ma Juliana sta provando direttamente che cosa significa per un corpo femminile impossessarsi dello spazio all'interno dell'apparato del programma spaziale. Il suo intento è quindi ben diverso. Per spingere fino in fondo l'analogia, possiamo dire che, nella sua logica scultorea, la Leite stia cercando la vagina del programma spaziale. Tratta lo *SHEE* nello stesso modo in cui tratta la vagina in *A Potential Space*: un'opera creata facendo lo stampo della vagina usando l'alginato, un materiale morbido specifico per i calchi del corpo. In senso filosofico, questo progetto impiegava un particolare metodo di calco del corpo per esaminare ciò che la vagina è in sé e per sé, piuttosto che per un altro: un pene, o fallo.

NS— Mi piace. Il suo programma artistico è il Female Space Program (programma spaziale femminile). Questo gioco di parole ci permette di parlare di una relazione femminile con un progetto statale tecnico-industriale fatto per colonizzare lo spazio esterno (di solito per conto degli uomini). Ma ci permette anche di affrontare l'esplorazione dell'elemento spaziale a livello di singoli corpi (femminili), cosa può essere raggiunto ad esempio. In quest'ultimo senso, forse il Male Space Program era l'arte tradizionale. Questa doppia implicazione illumina anche la distinzione tra incidente e rito. Ciò che è rito ci consegna dei diritti. L'accidente di avere un corpo femminile, ad esempio, si contrappone alla coreografia di un fallo galattico; l'erezione diventa quindi una protesi che spinge in fuori, verso le stelle. Uno strumento enorme.

Sembra dunque che il programma spaziale femminile non possa operare nello spazio vergine, perché l'idea di tale spazio è alla base del programma spaziale maschile. Il programma spaziale femminile deve riuscire allora a tracciarsi il proprio percorso attraverso l'invasione maschile dello spazio (*manspreading*); deve scavarsi la sua strada, trovare uno spazio potenziale all'interno di questo grande altro; all'interno di un *manspreading* che parte dalla tomba per arrivare alle stelle.

Penso che questo sia ciò che intendi, individuando la vagina del programma spaziale. E personalmente penso che questa nuova via (o programma) attraversi regioni che il programma spaziale maschile ha percorso, e le trovi disseminate di statue, eroi e membra. Si fa strada attraverso un terreno di immagini maschili, o manifestazioni figurative di uno spazio maschile (sculture di falli; sculture fatte da falli) e disvela un potenziale spazio per una scultura altra, in luoghi non riconosciuti come tali, in cui oggetti come i calchi vengono rivalutati.

DH— Esatto, come possiamo esplorare lo spazio senza limitarci soltanto a proiettare in esso qualsiasi ipotesi, desiderio o investimento che lì possa essere collocato? È esattamente questo il punto nel precedente lavoro della Leite, *A Potential Space*. Come si fa a sapere che forma ha una vagina, se non facendole assumere la forma di un divaricatore, un dildo, un pene? Oppone resistenza al farsi conoscere. Resta un nascondiglio (e un luogo nascosto).

Palpare lo spazio (gli spazi) è un'arte, come lo è conoscere il passato. In effetti, si potrebbe paragonare

il desiderio del diciottesimo secolo di possedere
l'antichità alla moderna corsa allo spazio.

NS__ La mostra *Orogenesi* ha luogo tra gli
oggetti rinvenuti nella Villa dei Papiri: una collezione
domestica d'alta borghesia che include busti di filosofi,
poeti, e così via. Pertanto, le sculture della Leite sono
installate all'interno di un pantheon di figure storiche
e allegoriche. Mentre il suo motivo è, in un certo
senso, formale (alcune sculture nascono da processi
algoritmici, basati su ripetizioni e regole), sussiste
comunque un invito al mito e all'allegoria. Il fatto che
dopo aver scavato tra gli strati i visitatori dovrebbero
scoprire un programma spaziale femminile, uno spazio
interiore, dimostra che il progetto della Leite non è in
alcun modo classicheggiante. A volte le affermazioni
artistiche più contemporanee hanno luogo in un
museo pieno di vecchi marmi. Per quanto possiamo
ammirare le forme equilibrate e levigate delle sculture
di Villa dei Papiri e osservarle pulsare con la sacralità
dell'Olimpo, la ripetizione e la frammentazione della
Leite monumentalizzano nuovamente il corpo. La
Leite si rivolge alla temporalità fugace del corpo - un
essere che è visibile solo parzialmente durante ogni
azione data. Il suo lavoro suggerisce un corpo finito
in una rappresentazione incompiuta. Questa estetica
rievoca molto più di quel particolare corpo: più corpi
a venire, e più incarnazione. Orogenesi non è soltanto
un'attivazione della collezione del museo nazionale,
quanto piuttosto una vera e propria dichiarazione
fondamentale sull'occupazione dello spazio...

DH__ Sì. Ma ora voglio tornare alle montagne in
movimento, all'orogenesi. Qui c'è anche una riflessione
sul nostro rapporto con la forza: le forze naturali,
la potenza tecnologica, l'azione del nostro corpo.
L'Orogenesi della Leite è una danza di ricettività delle
forze che ci sovrastano. È il peso della materia e della
Storia sui nostri corpi. Giocando con l'interrogativo di
come ci poniamo di fronte alle minacce, questo lavoro
dimostra l'importanza della resistenza in rapporto al
mantenimento della massa muscolare, letteralmente
e figurativamente. La differenza tra la montagna e il
vulcano è che il vulcano ha sempre il potenziale per il
cambiamento dall'interno, al contrario della montagna,
che erode dall'esterno. C'è qualcosa di suggestivo, nel
vulcano, per la pratica della Leite, in quanto è strano,
per uno scultore, scavarsi la propria via attraverso la
massa di materia, piuttosto che scalpellarla dall'esterno.
La pratica scultorea della Leite opera all'interno della
zona di subduzione, nel terreno instabile della scultura,
dove c'è sempre la possibilità di un nuovo divenire.

Mario Codognato__

è stato sin dalla sua fondazione il curatore capo
del MADRE, Napoli. Ha curato anche progetti di
arte contemporanea presso il Museo Archeologico
Nazionale di Napoli, con le mostre di Francesco
Clemente (2002), Jeff Koons (2003), Anish Kapoor
(2003), Richard Serra (2004), Anselm Kiefer (2004) e
la prima retrospettiva museale su Damien Hirst (2004).
Dal 2014 al 2016 è stato il curatore capo della 21er
Haus del Belvedere di Vienna.

Dehlia Hannah__

è filosofa e curatrice, attualmente ricercatrice post-
doc con la borsa di studio Mads Øvlisen presso il
Dipartimento di Chimica e Bioscienze dell'Università
di Aalborg-Copenaghen; è un'affiliata del Laboratory
for Past Disaster Studies presso l'Università di
Aarhus e la School of Earth and Space Exploration
presso l'Arizona State University. Ha conseguito un
dottorato di ricerca in Filosofia presso la Columbia
University, con specializzazioni in Filosofia della
Scienza ed Estetica.

Nadim Samman__

è curatore e storico dell'arte. Ha studiato Filosofia
al University College di Londra prima di conseguire
il dottorato di ricerca al Courtauld Institute of Art.
Ha co-fondato la prima Biennale Antarctica (2017)
e l'Antarctic Pavilion (Venezia, 2015-). Nel 2016 ha
curato la 5 ° Biennale Internazionale di Mosca per la
Giovane Arte e nel 2012 la 4° Biennale di Marrakech
(con Carson Chan).

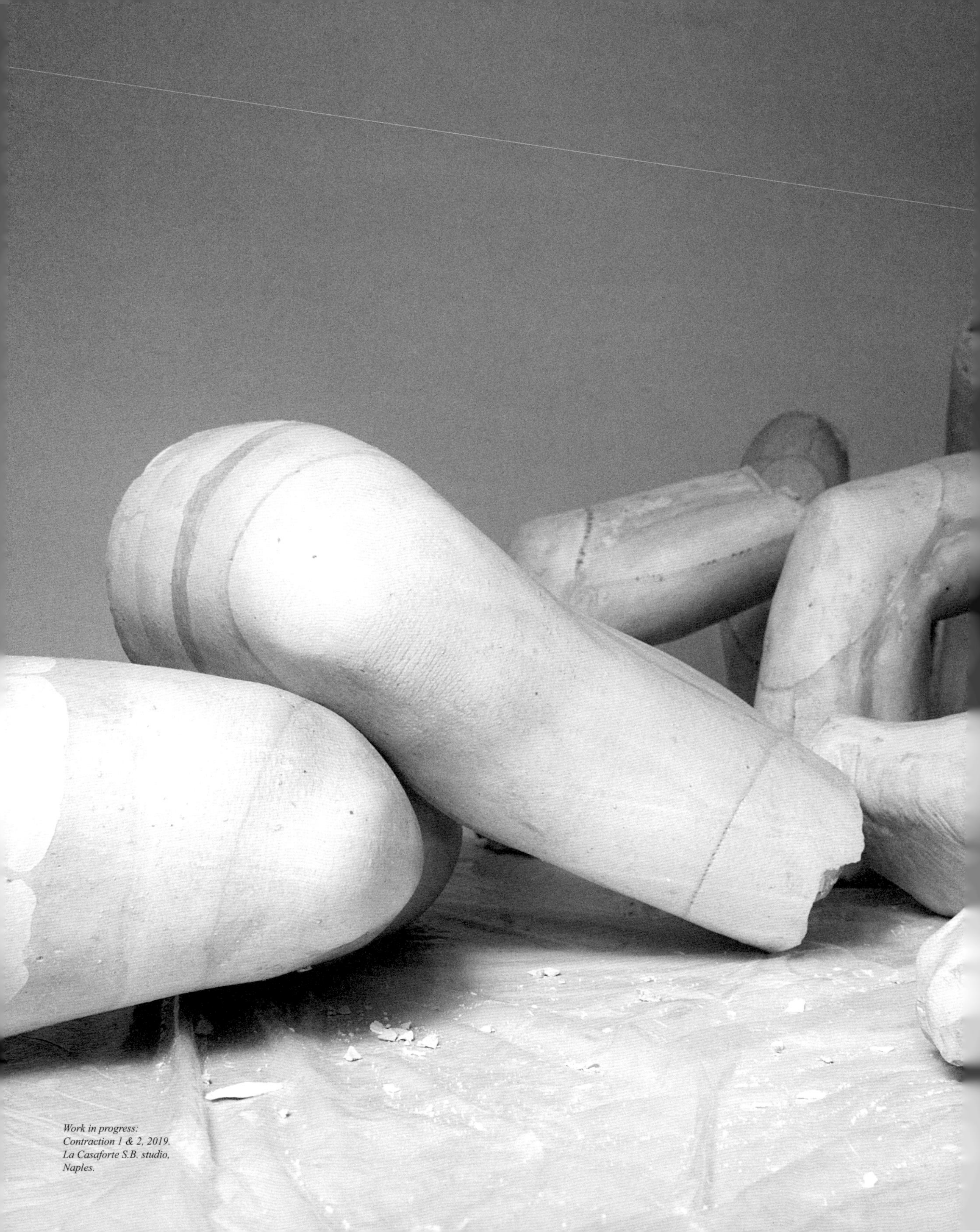

Work in progress:
Contraction 1 & 2, 2019.
La Casaforte S.B. studio,
Naples.

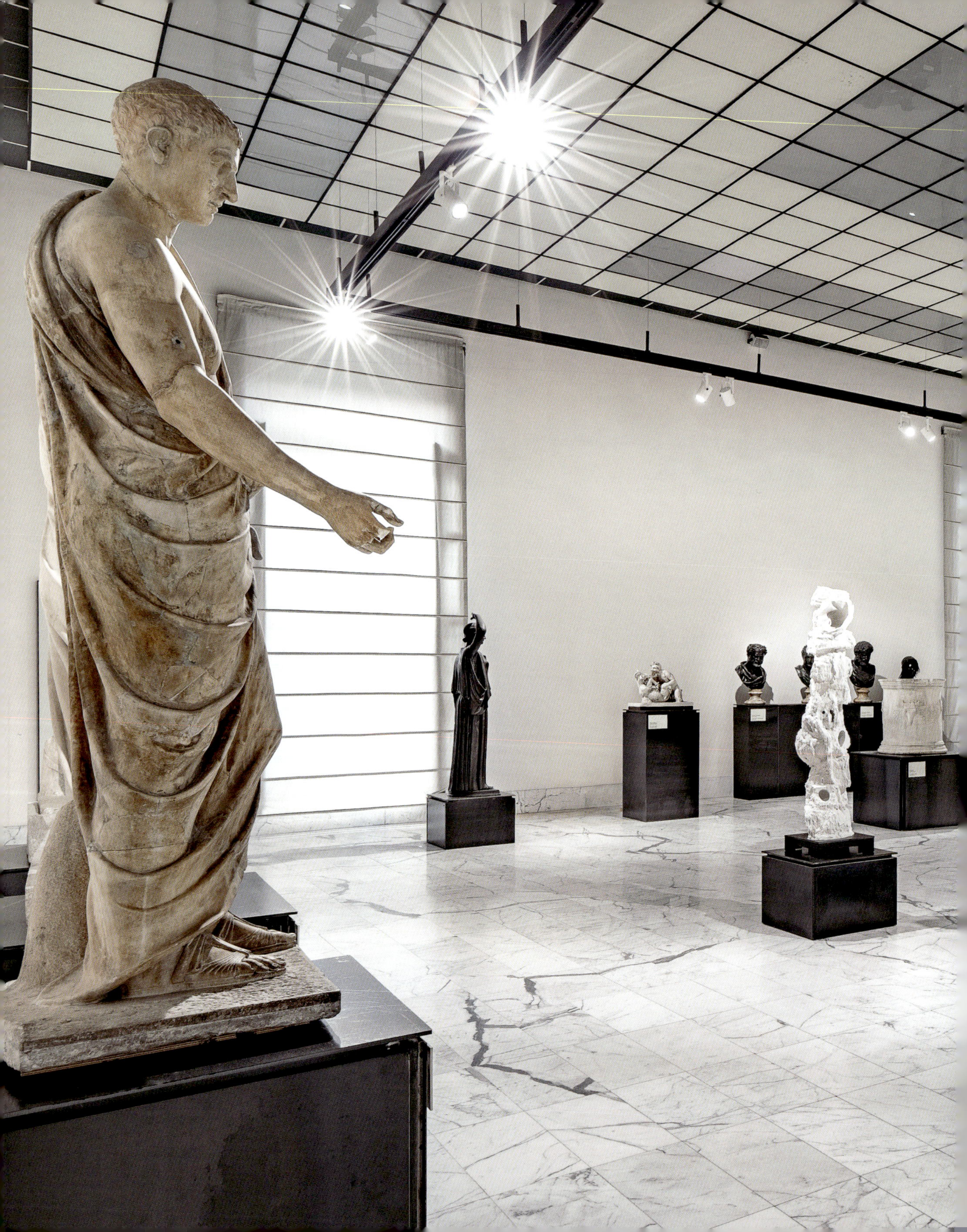

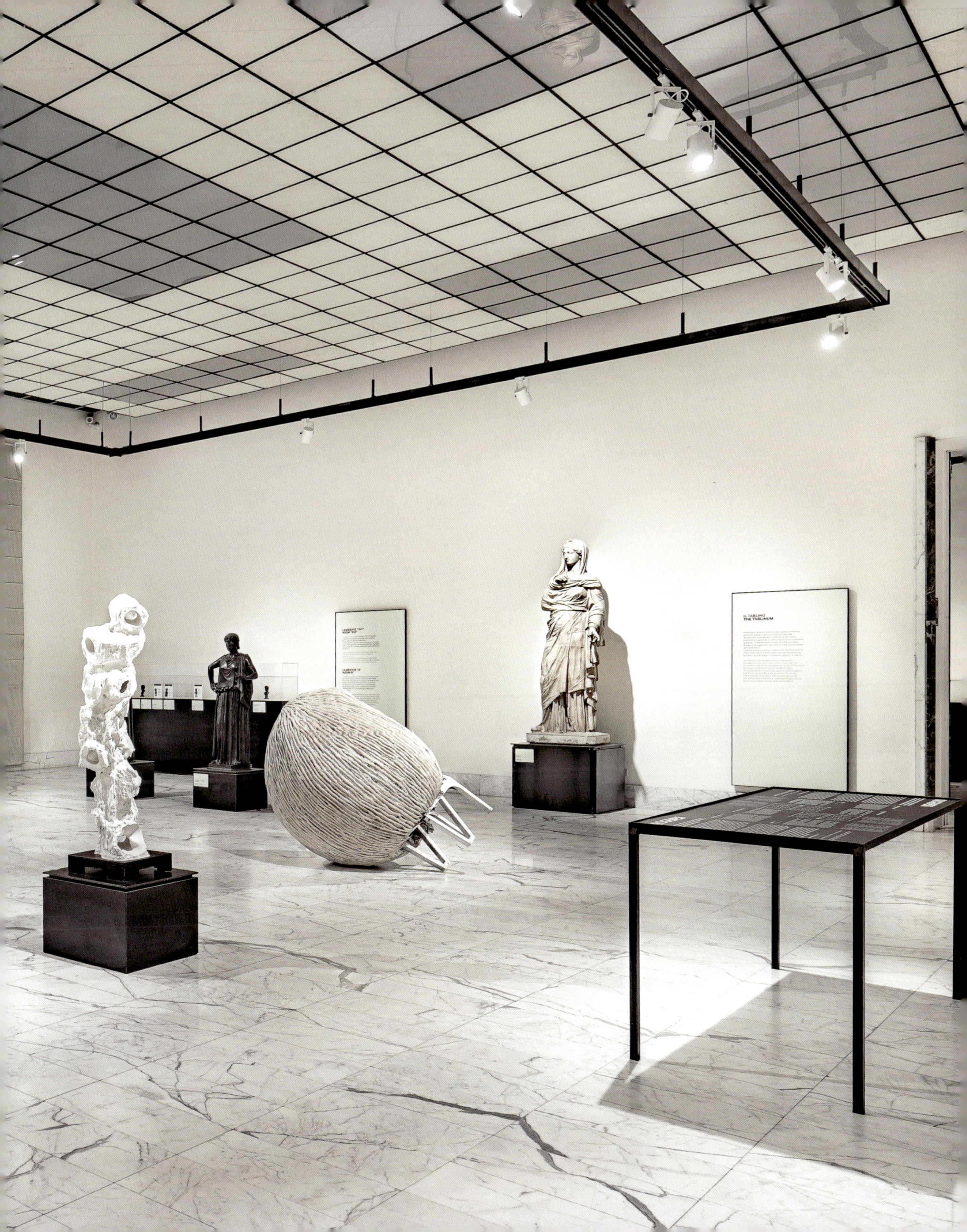

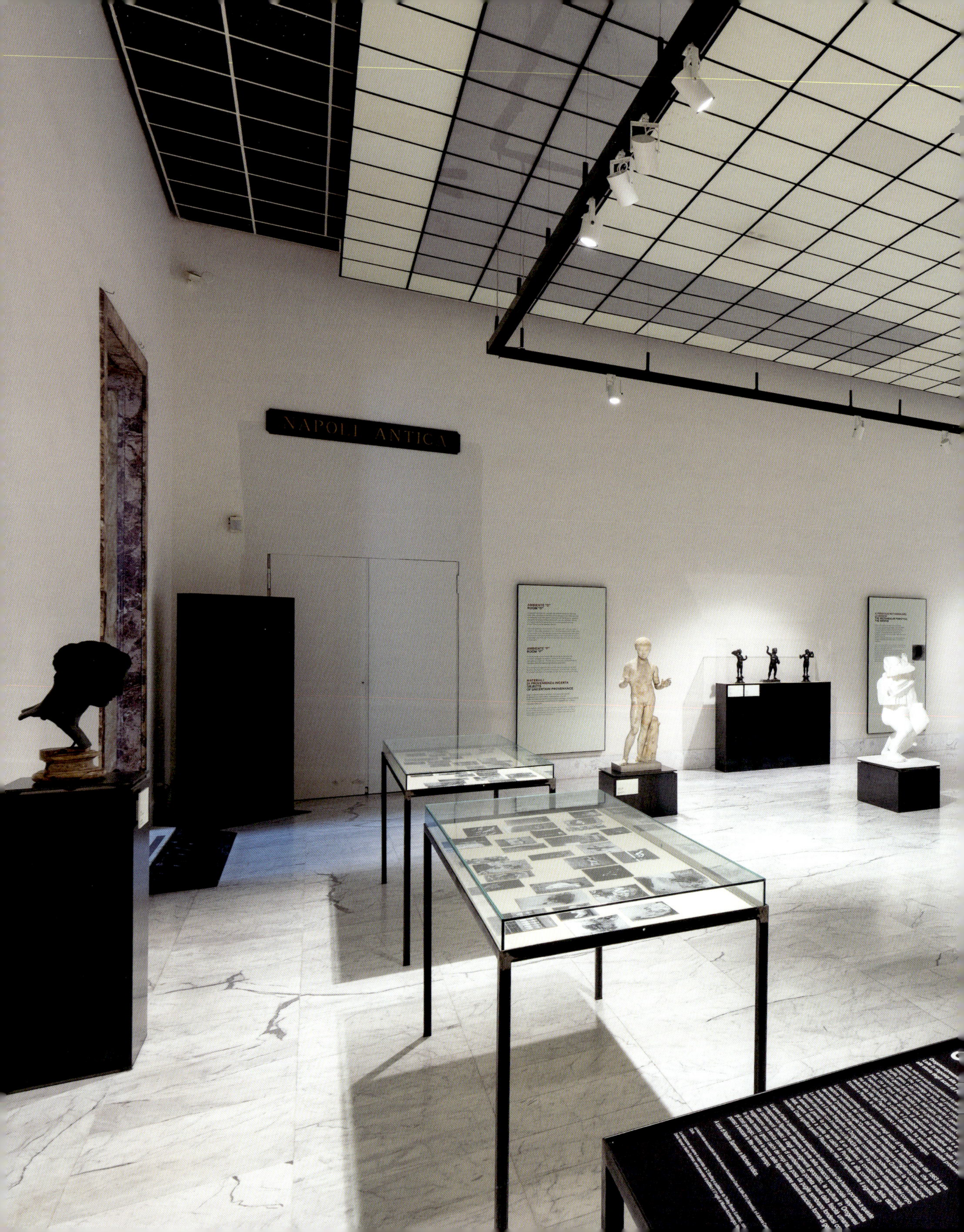

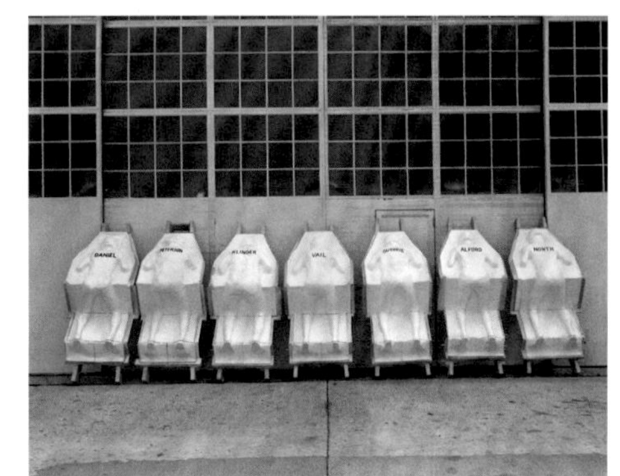

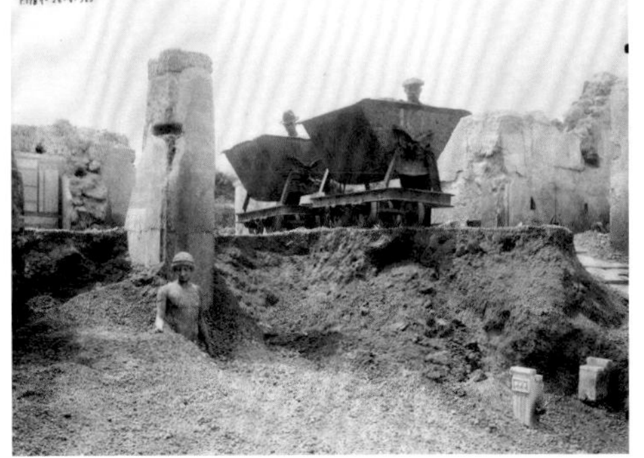

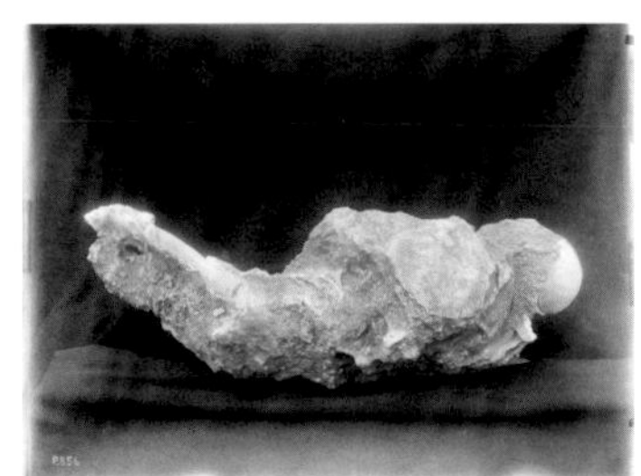

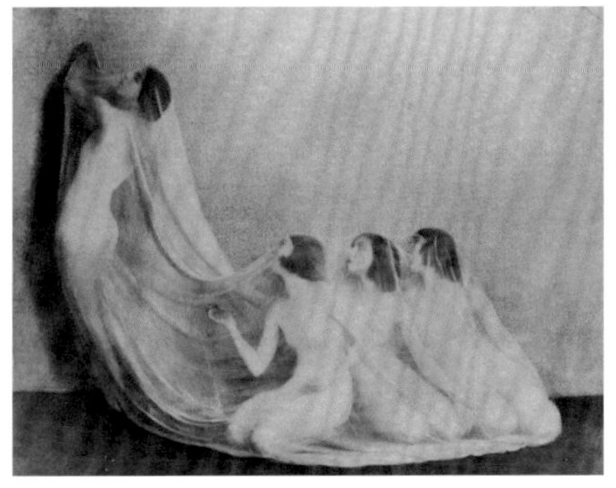

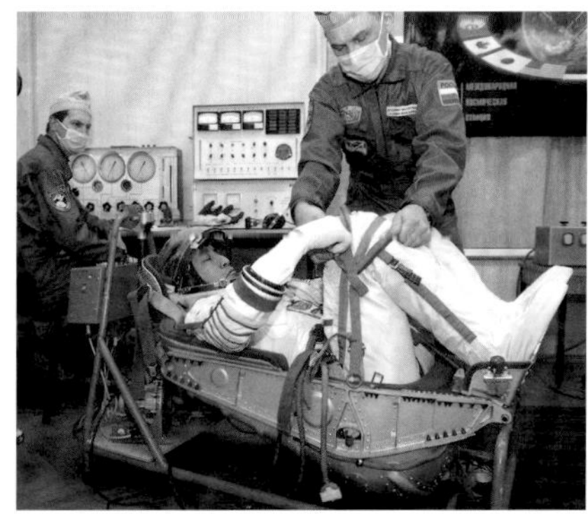

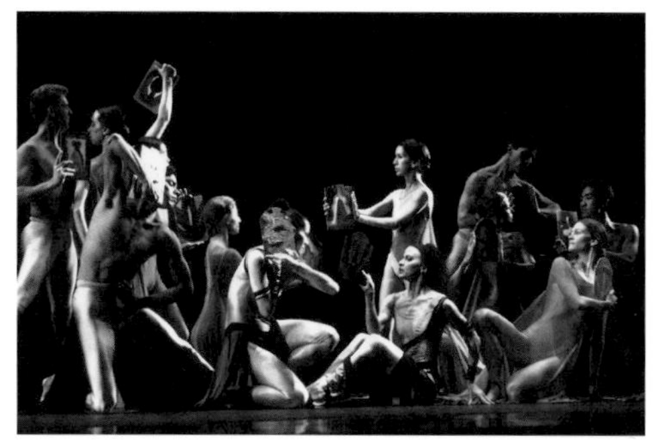
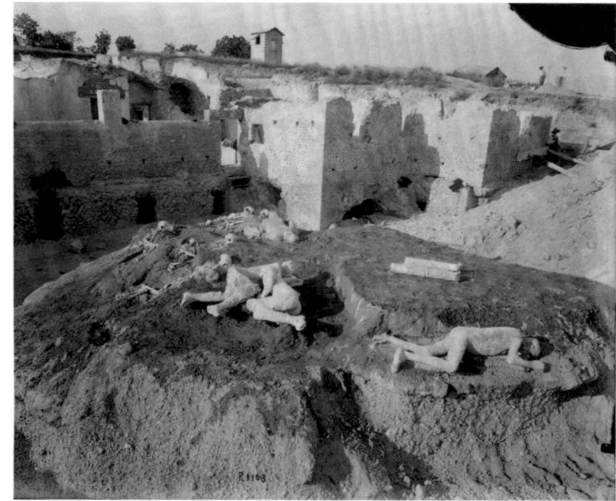
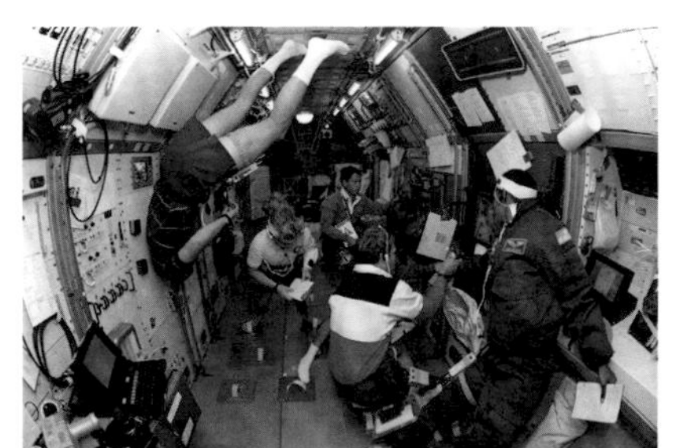
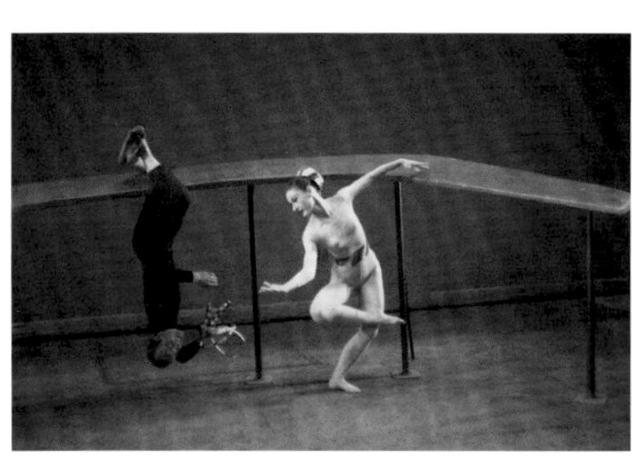
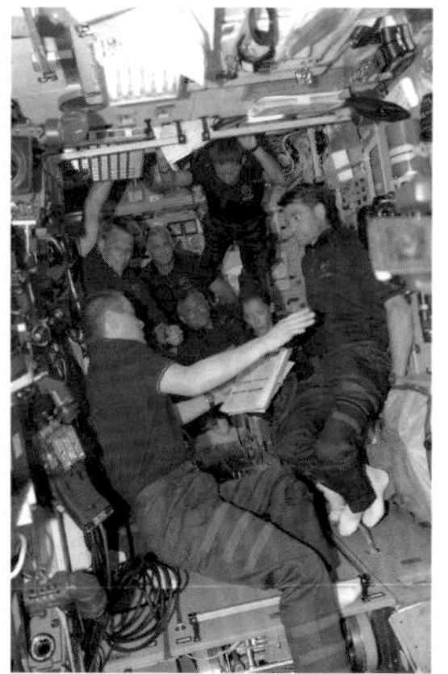
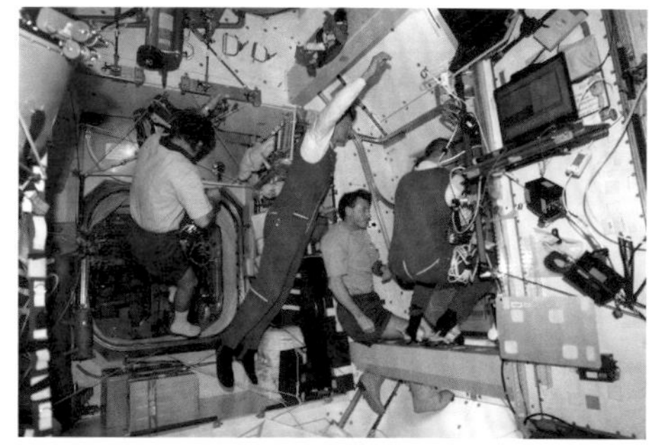
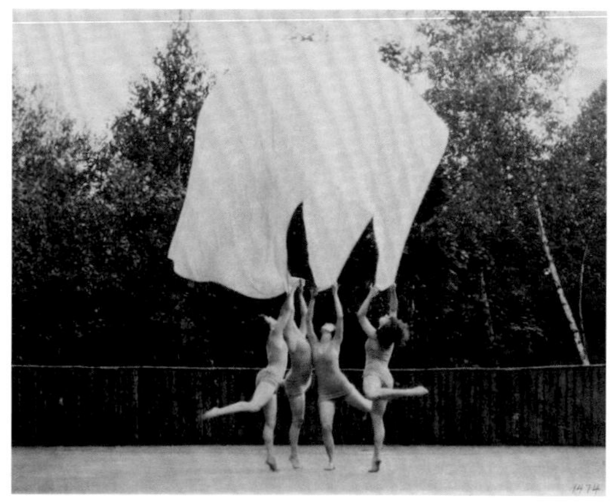

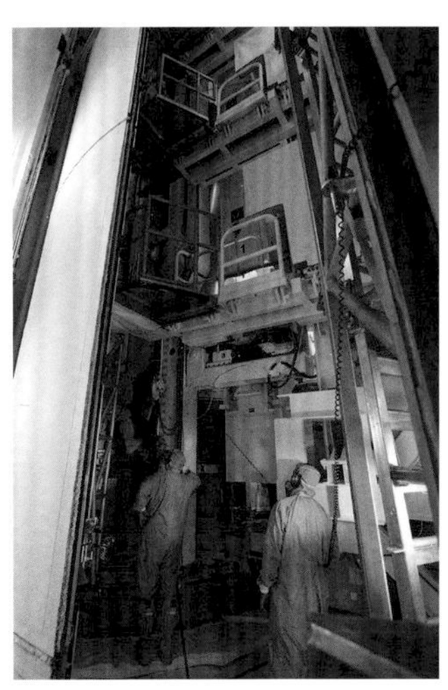
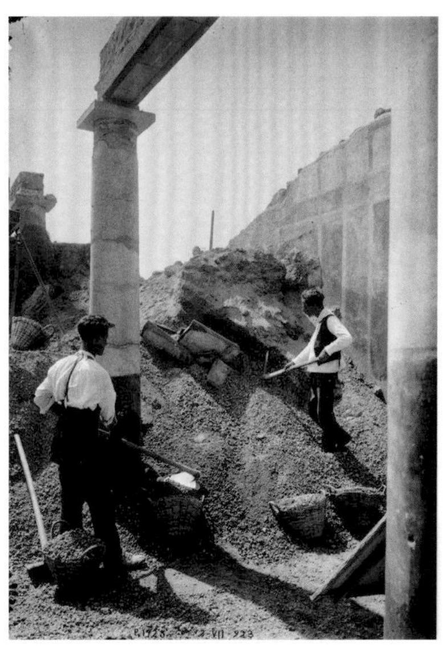
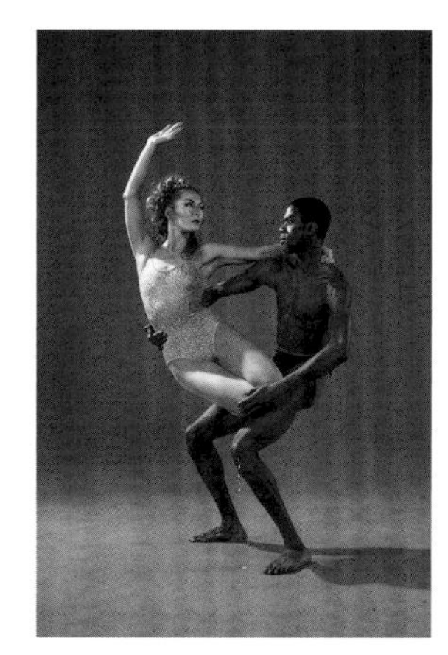
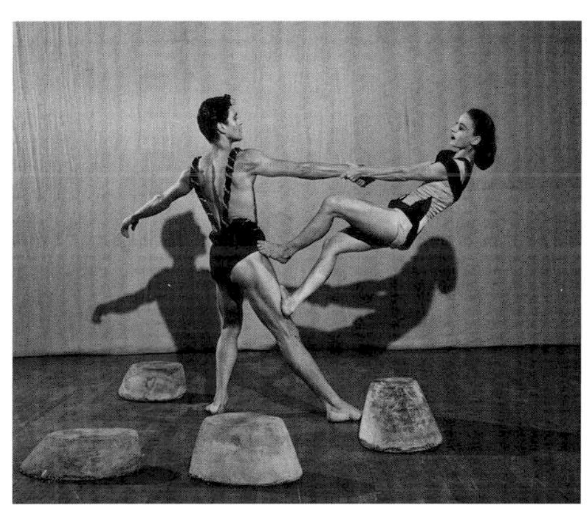
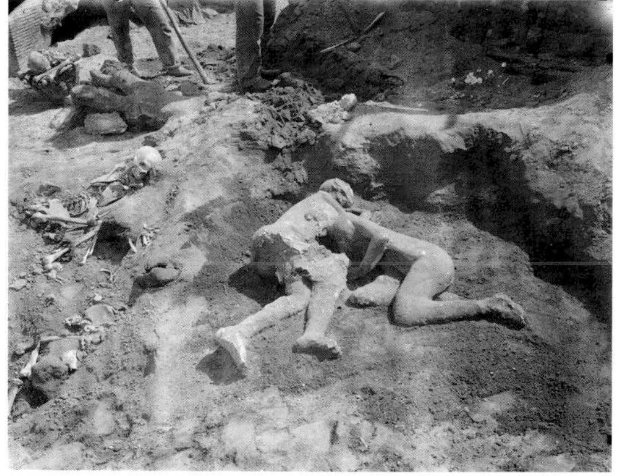
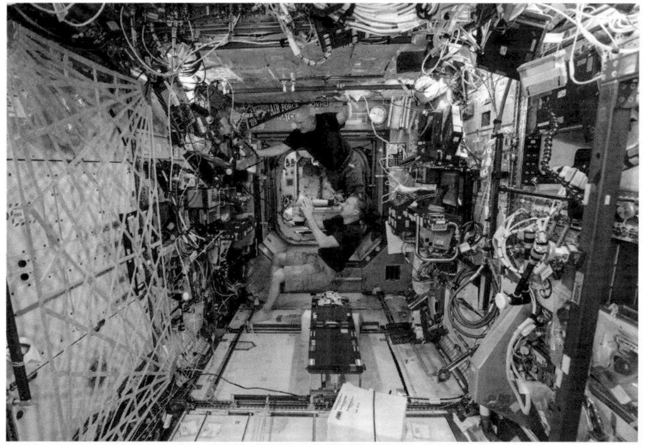

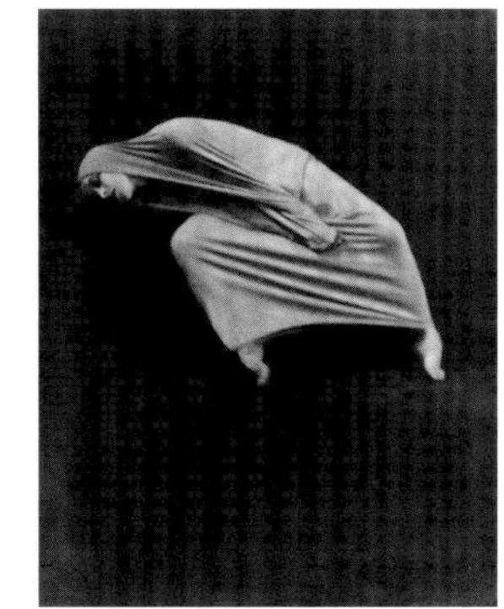
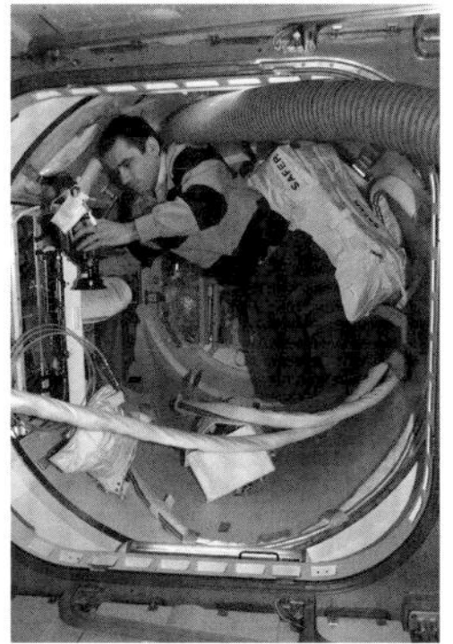
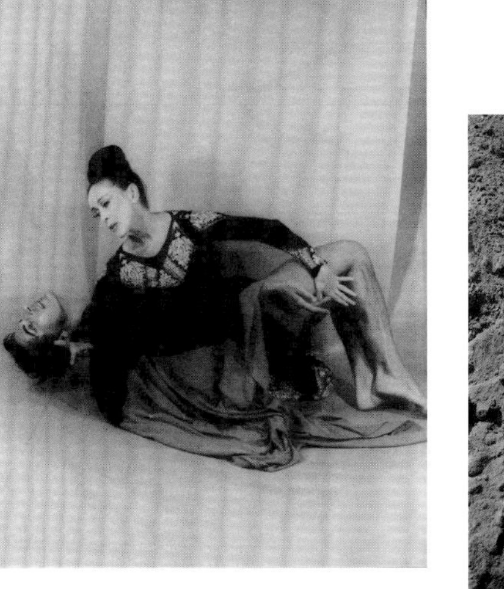
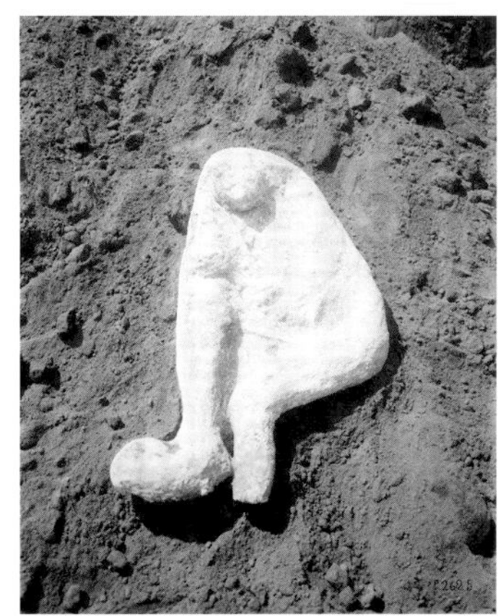
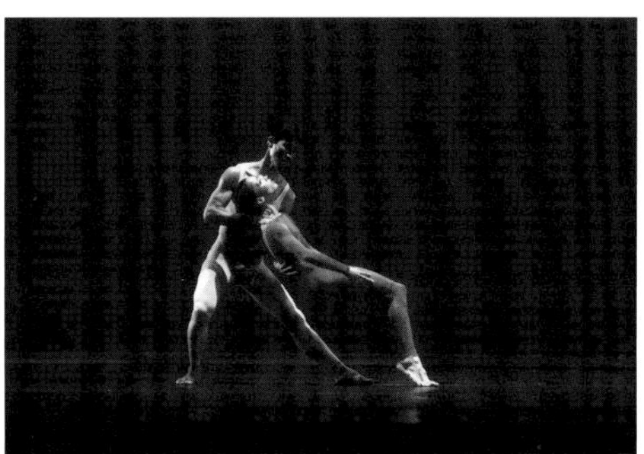
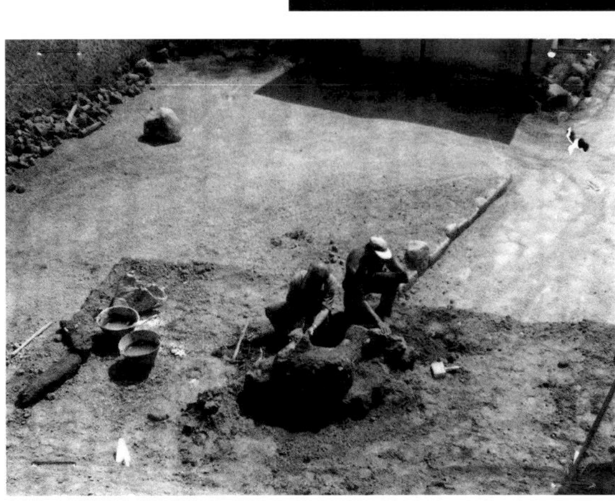
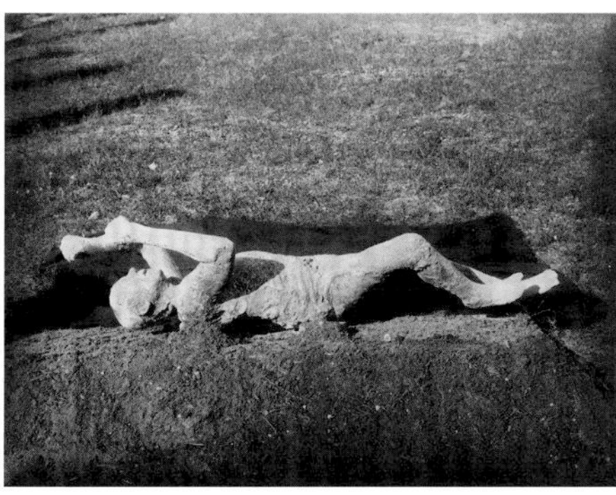
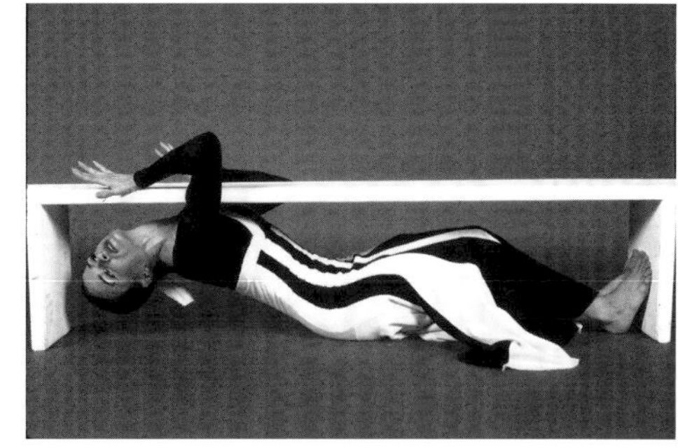

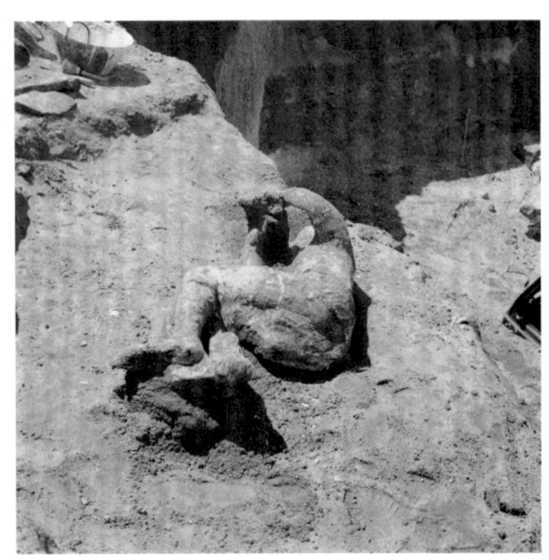
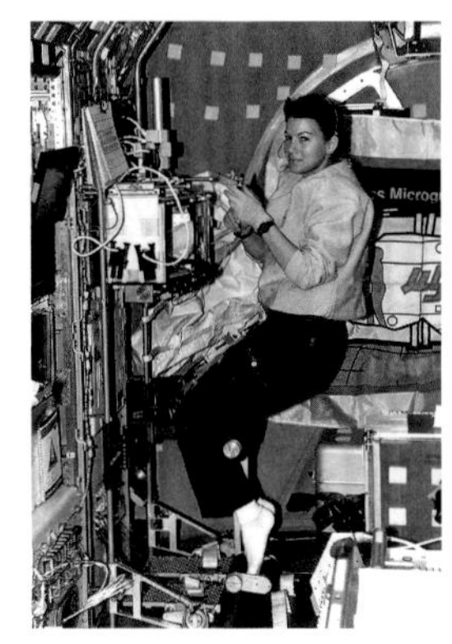
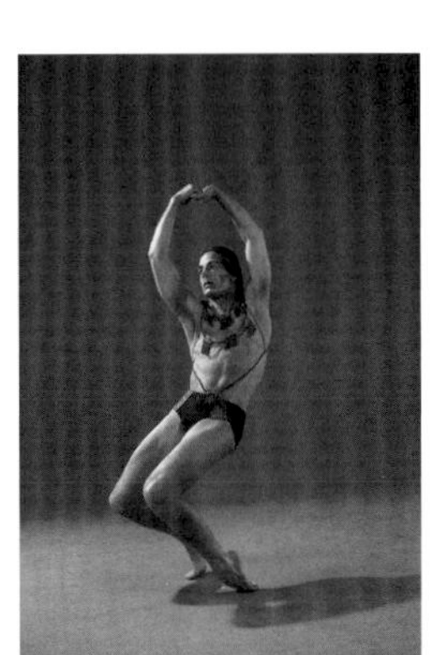
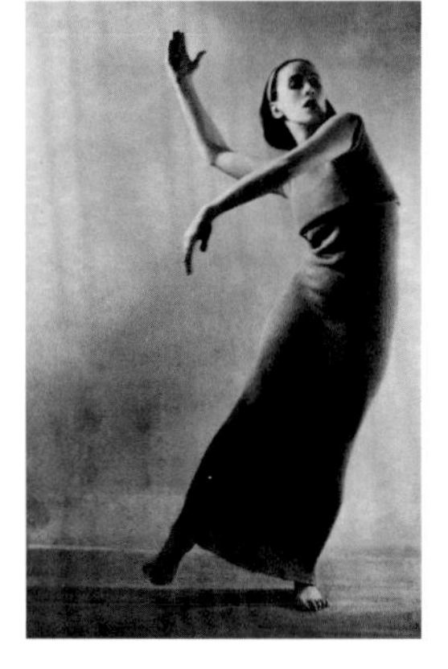
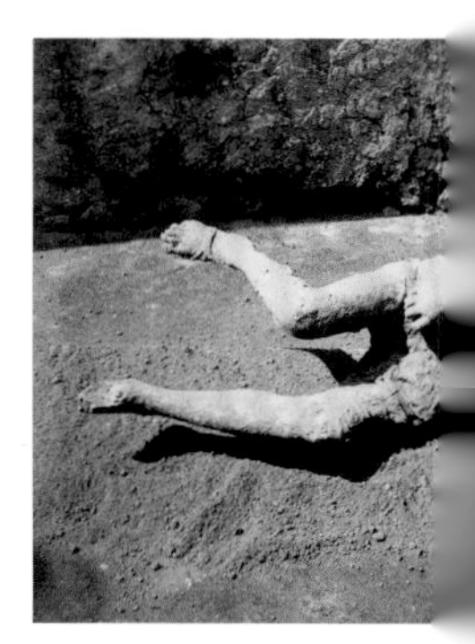
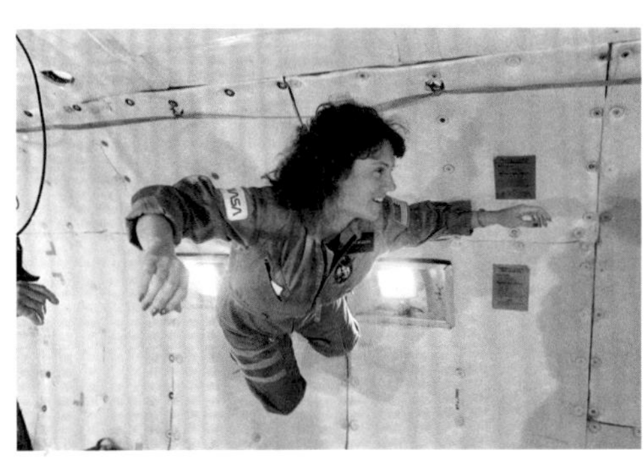
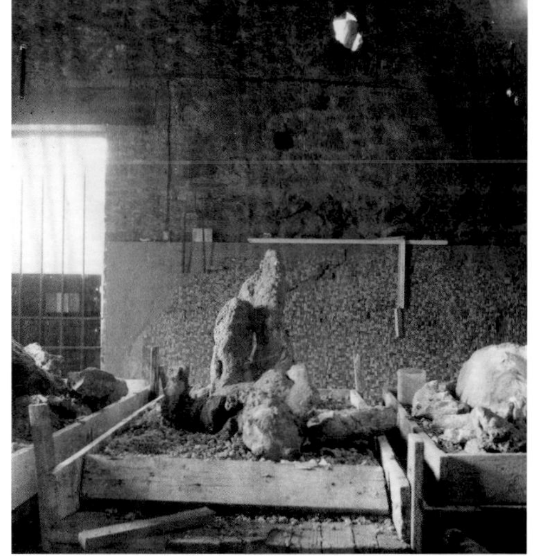
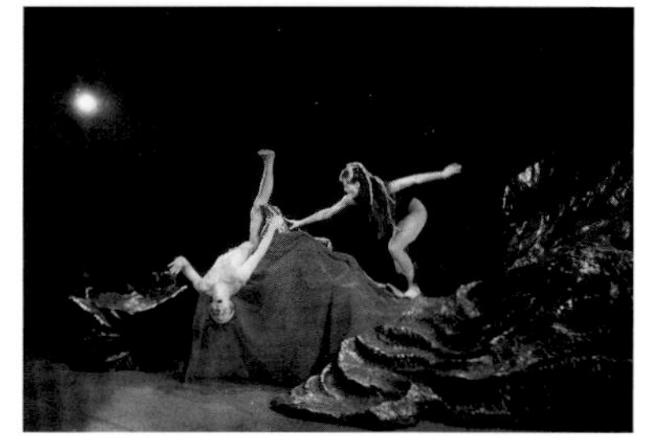

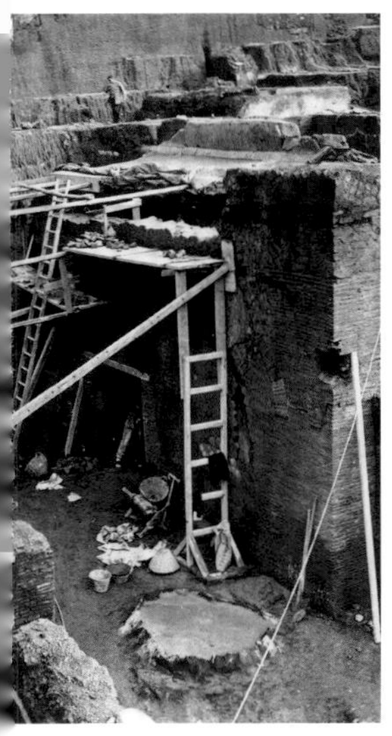
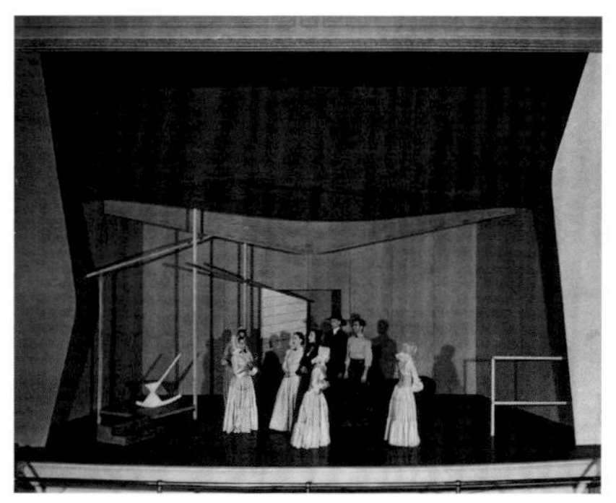
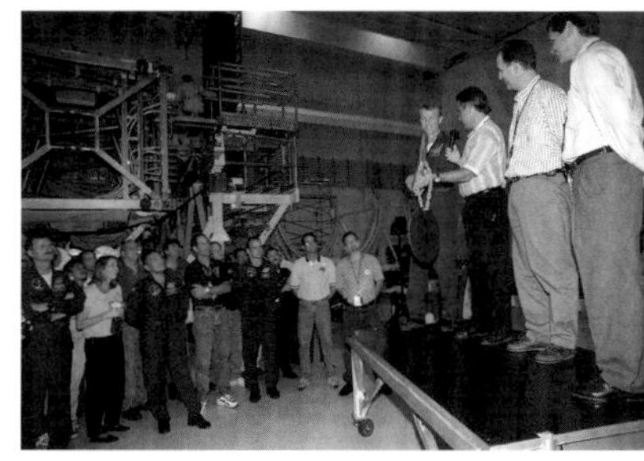
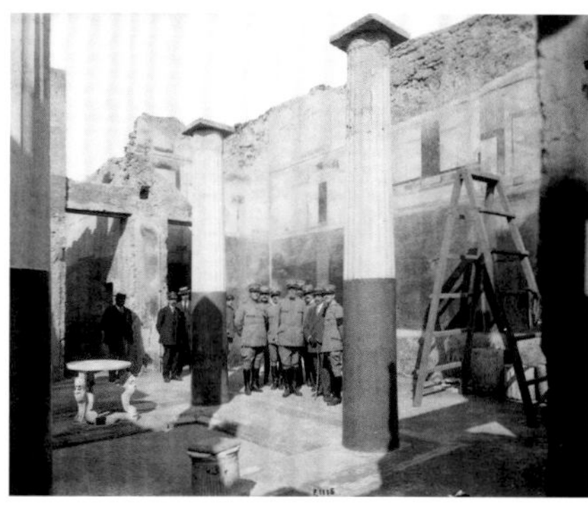
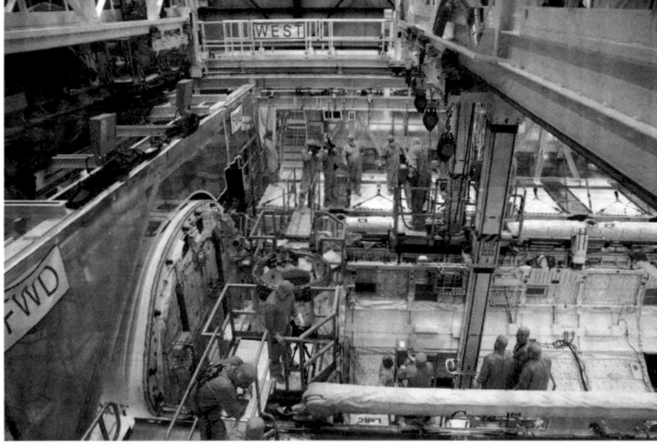
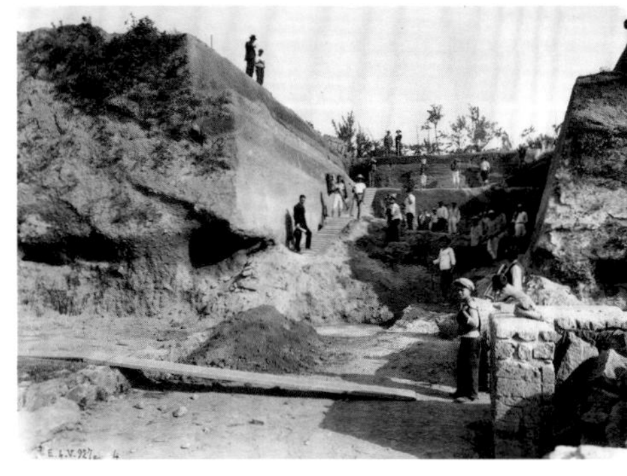
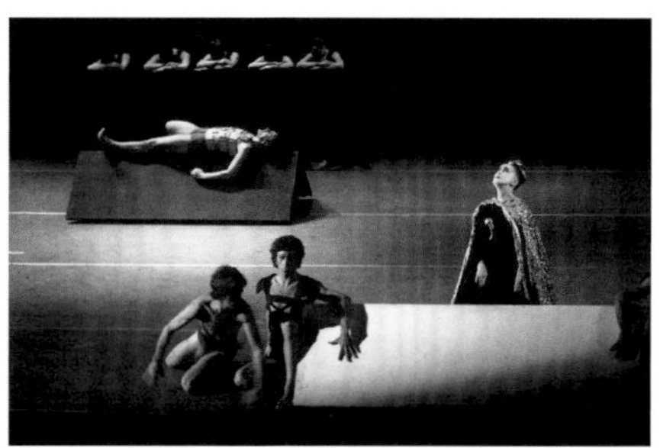

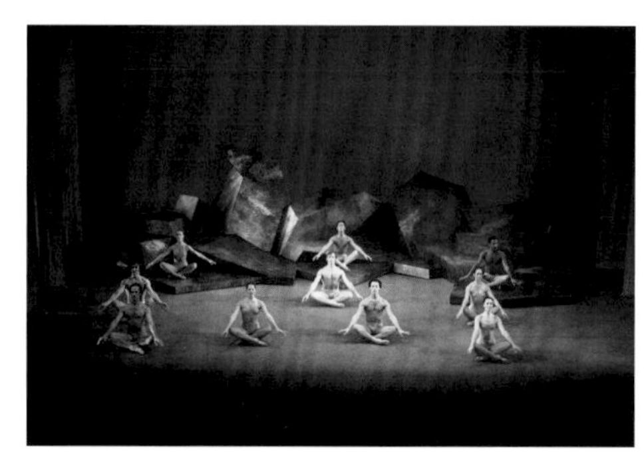
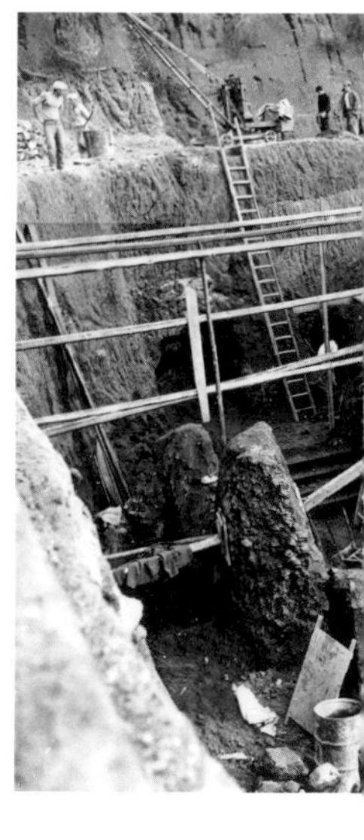
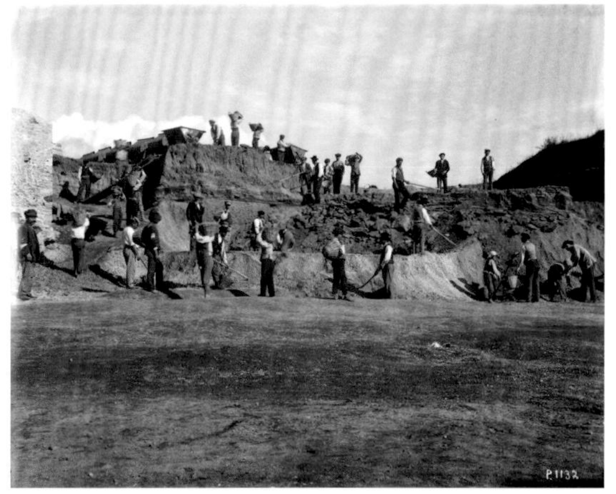
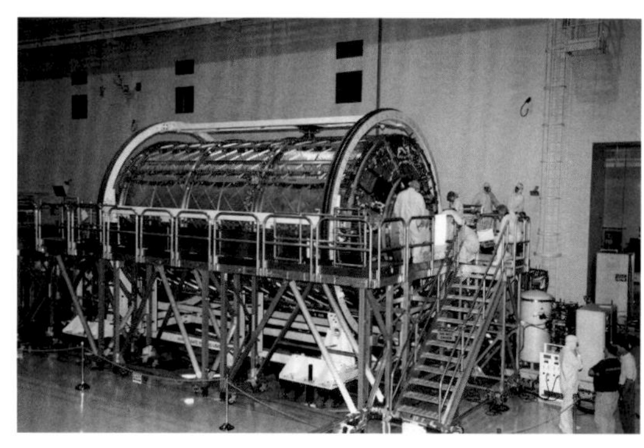
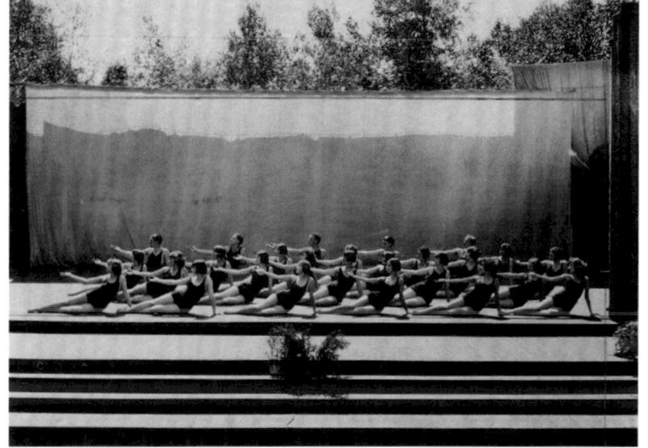
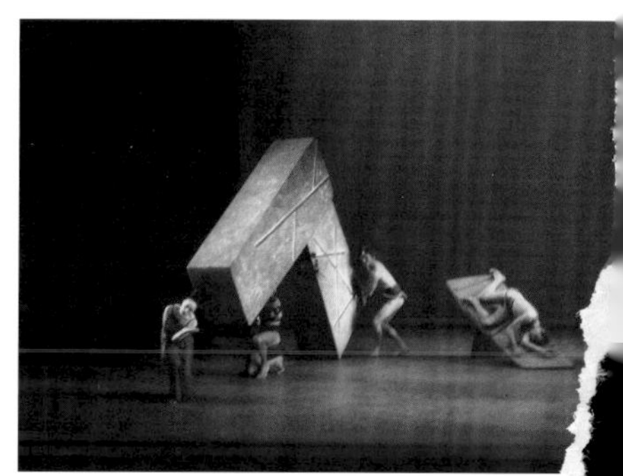
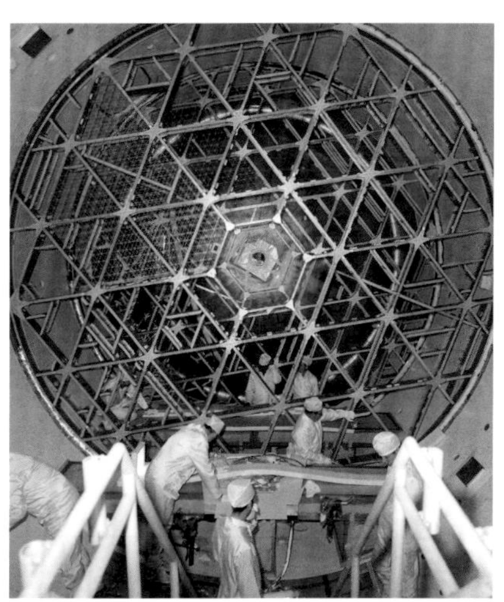
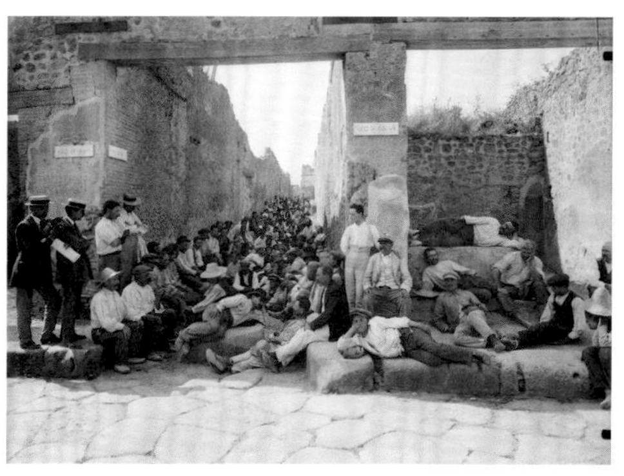

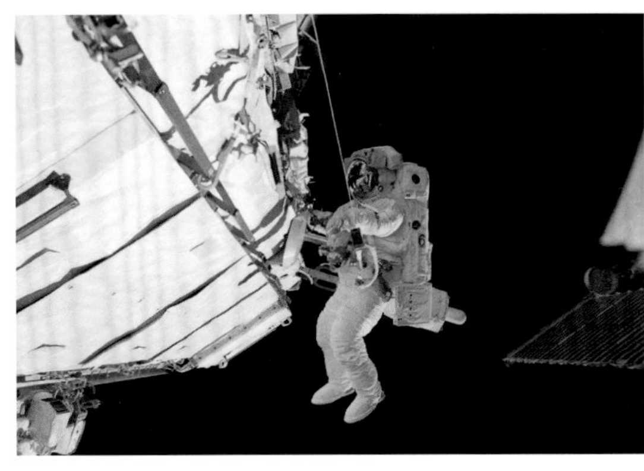
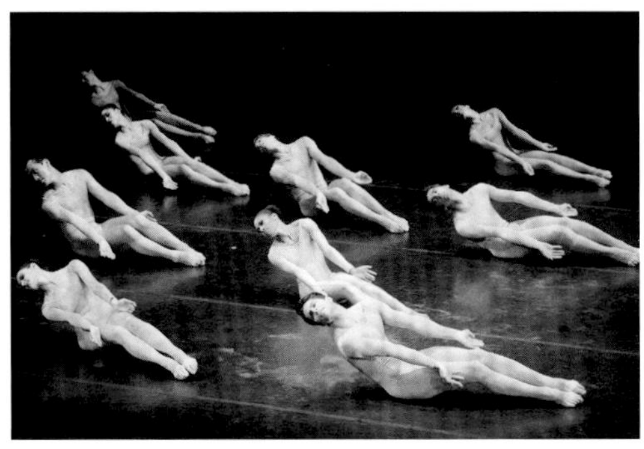
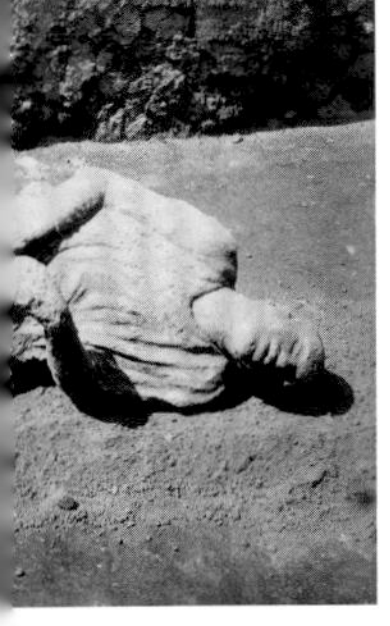
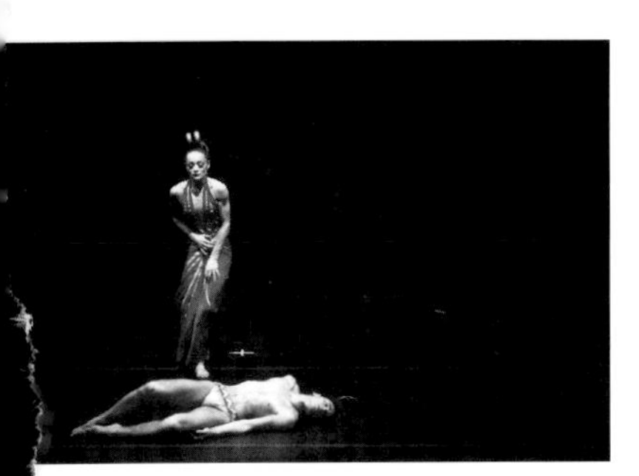
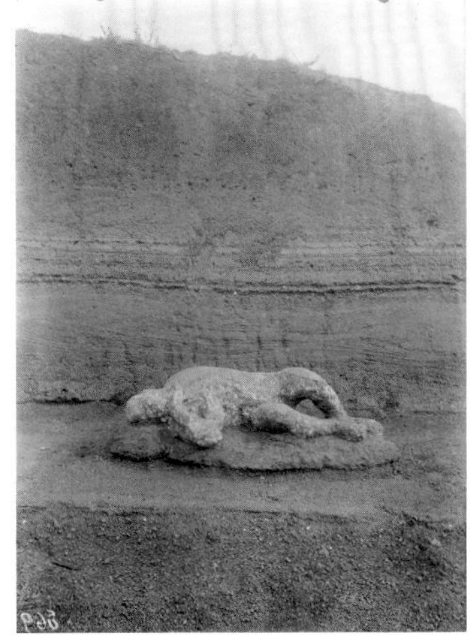
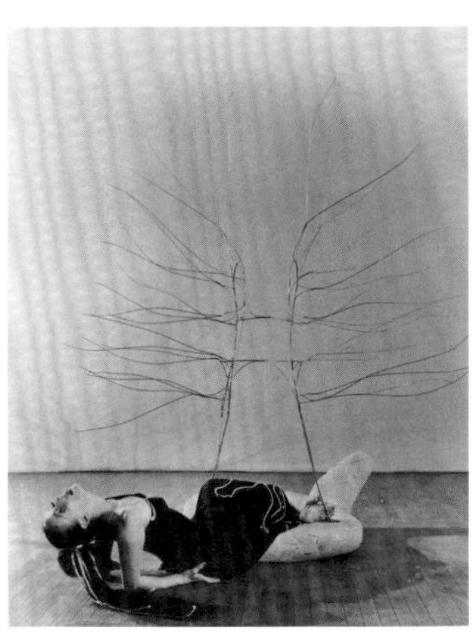
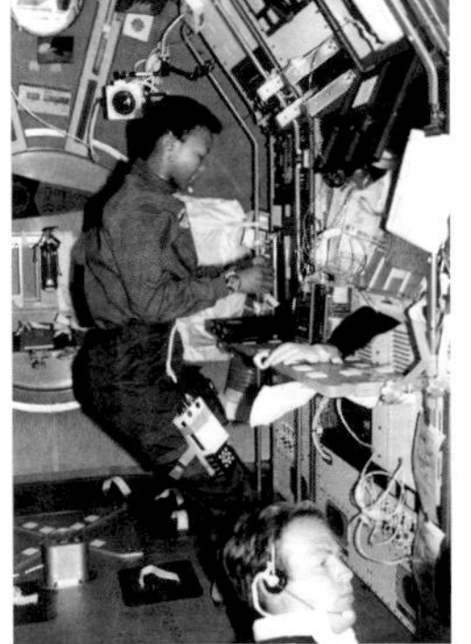
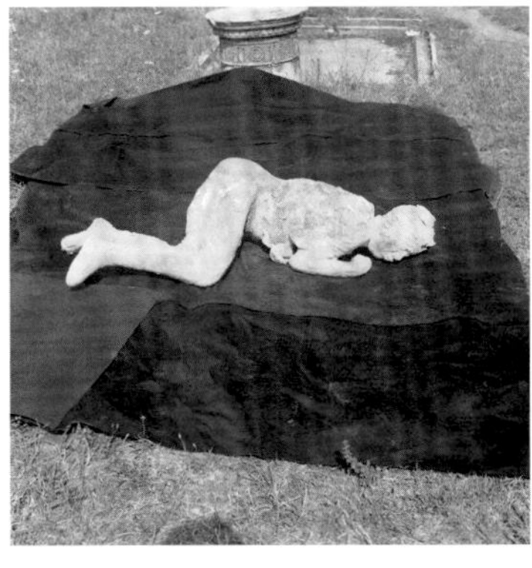
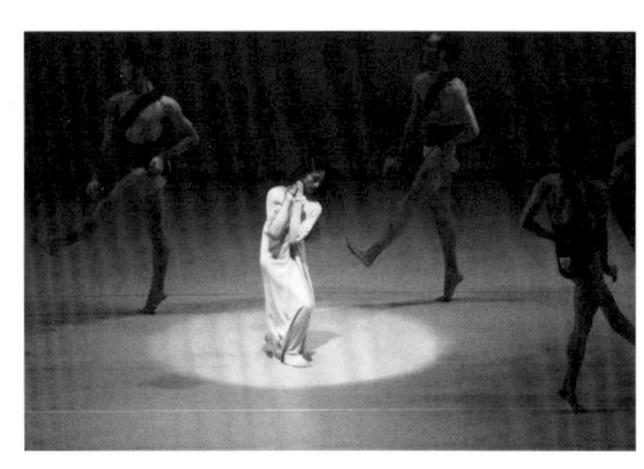

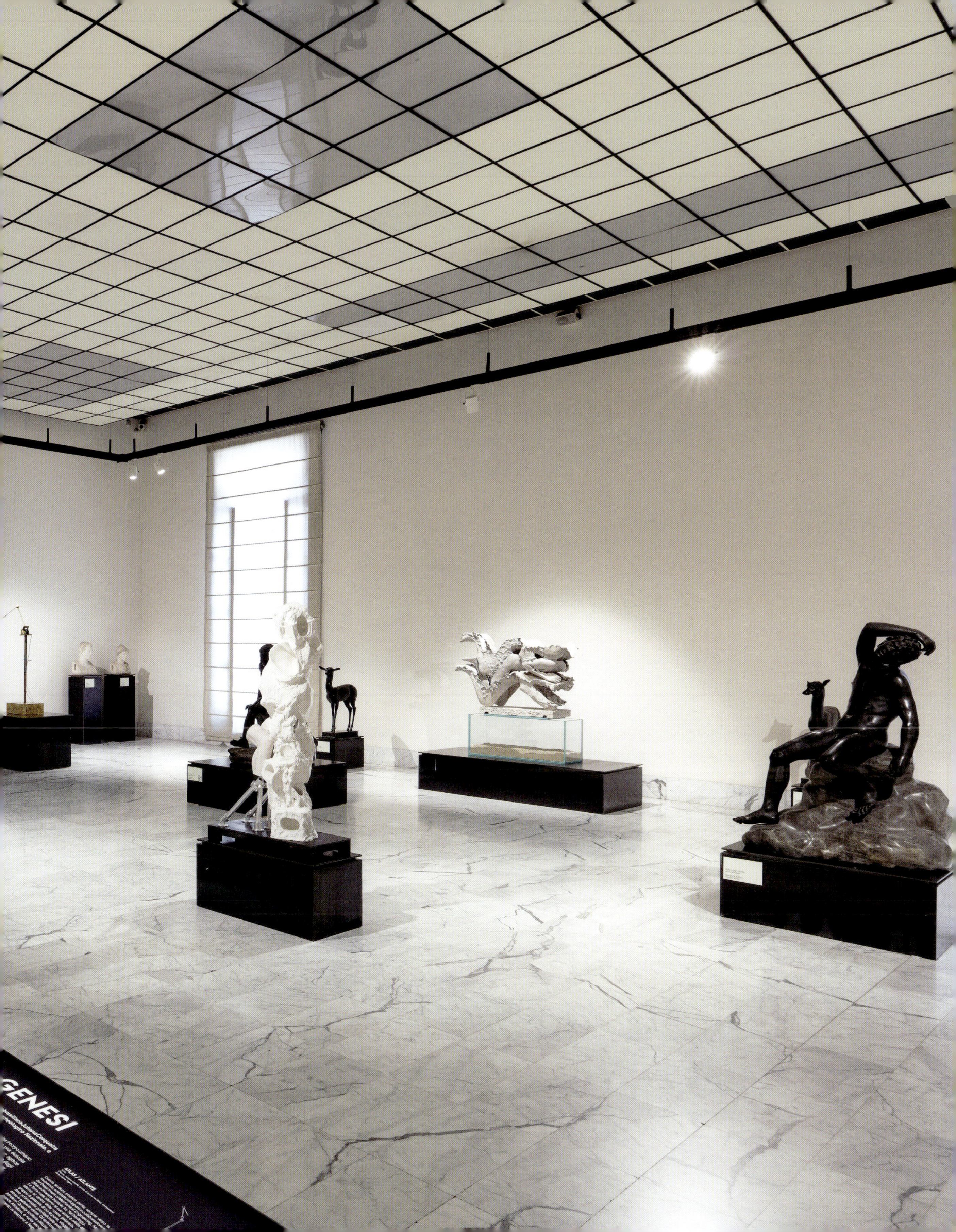
GENESI
ATLAS / ATLANTE

In 1986 NASA published their Manned
System Integration Standards handbook
for the design of workstations and habitats
for outer space. The research leading to
this publication involved several studies
measuring the human body, including a
'grasp-reach' study. In this study a person
strapped to a model space faring chair
(such as those used in the NASA Space
Shuttle) would reach as far as they could
in all directions, describing the area within
their reach while sitting down. This was
the area within which NASA could then
place controls and buttons to be operated
by the astronaut strapped to this chair
during take-off or other maneuvers. For
this sculpture Cerqueira Leite reenacted
NASA's grasp reach study within a large,
clay-lined mold, while sitting on a model
of NASA's Space Shuttle chair. The
resulting spherical sculpture not only
demonstrates the artist's reach, but re-
defines the borders and form of her body
as action.

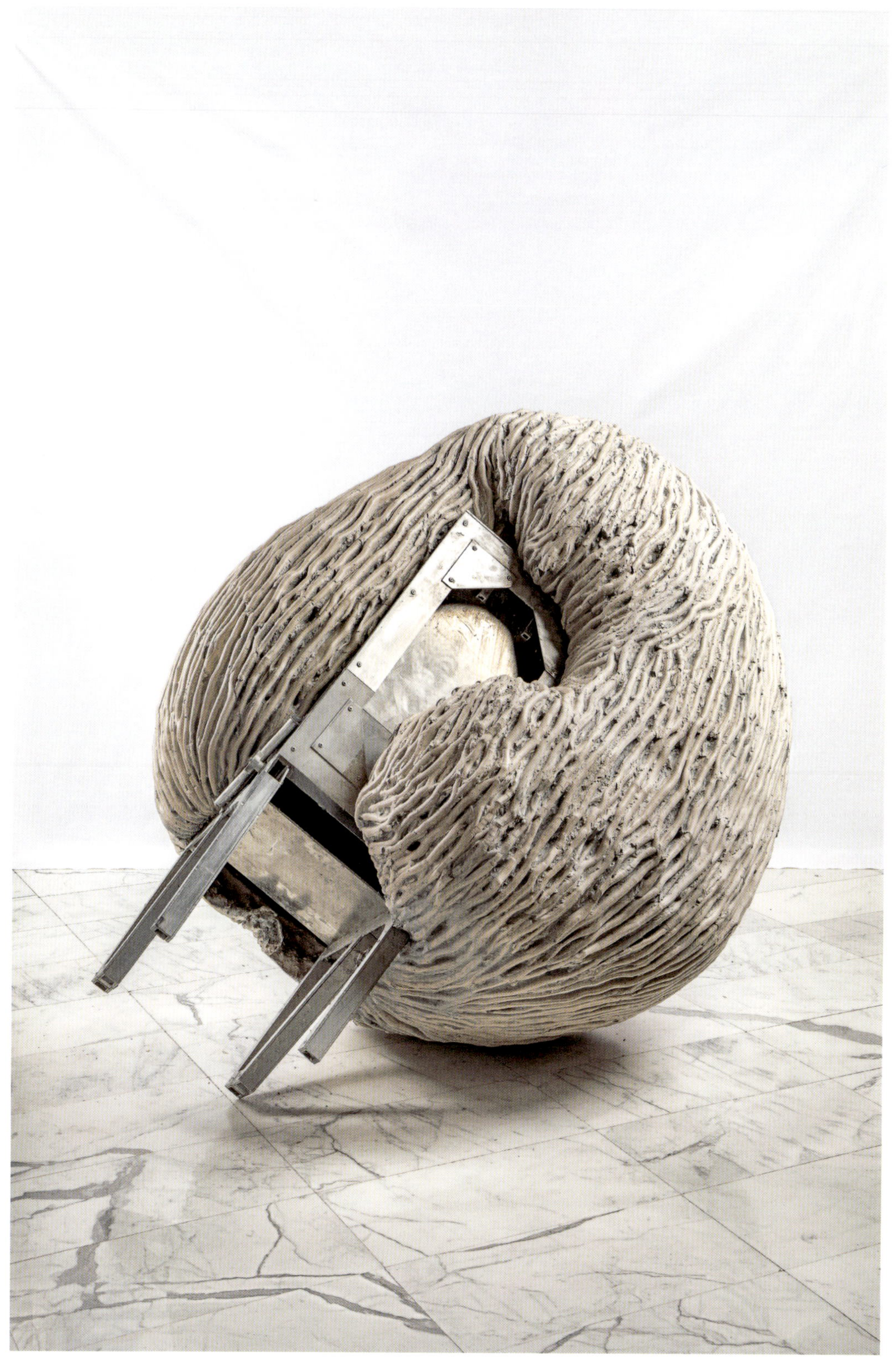

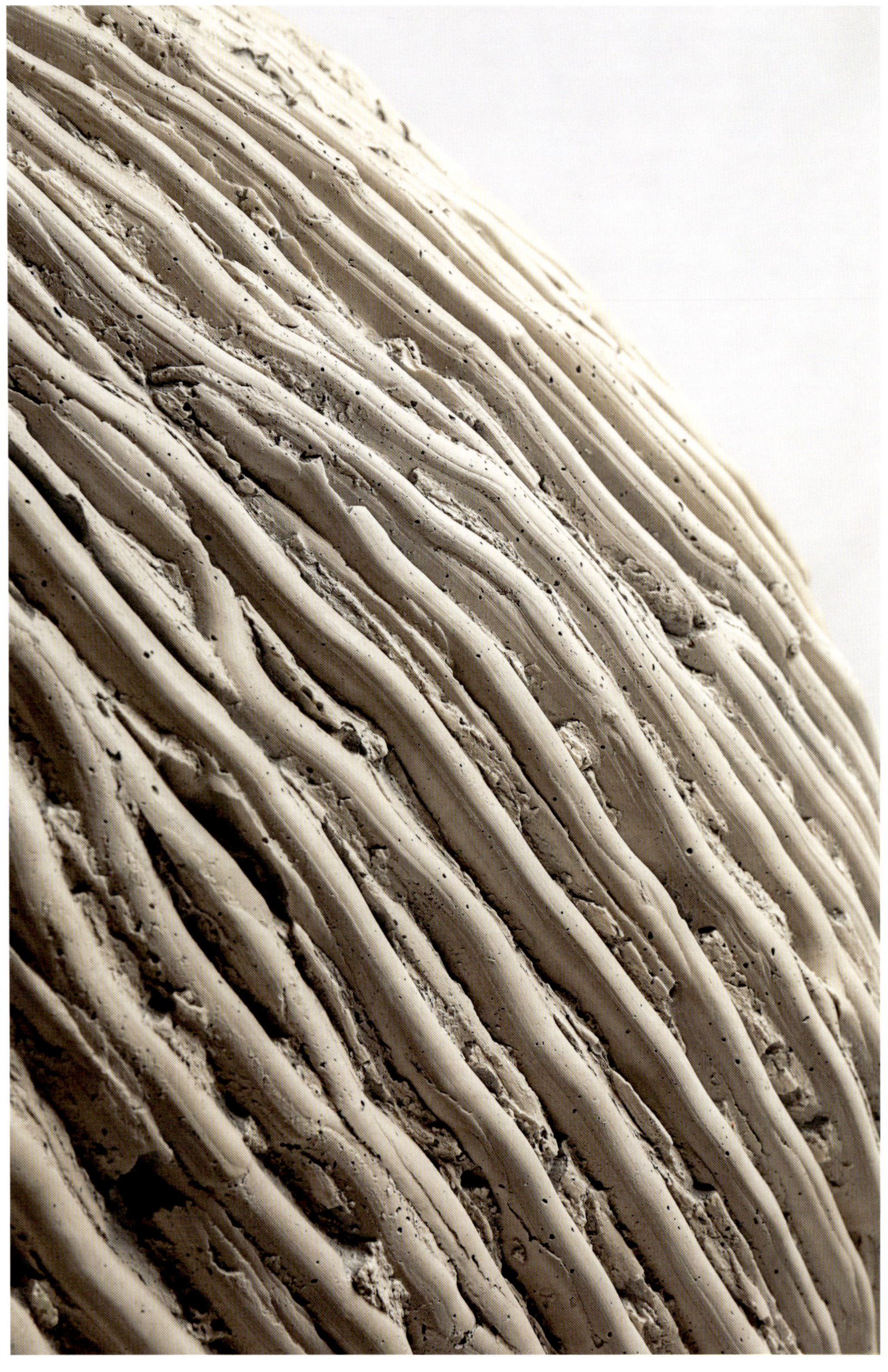

Nal 1986 la NASA ha pubblicato il manuale
Manned System Integration Standards,
una guida per la realizzazione di interfacce
e ambienti nello spazio. La ricerca che ha
portato a questa pubblicazione si compone
di diversi studi sulle misurazioni del corpo,
tra i quali in particolare un'analisi sui limiti
di estensione del braccio umano. Questo
studio si svolse osservando la massima area
descritta da ciò che una persona saldamente
legata a un sedile (simile a quelli utilizzati
sullo Space Shuttle) riusciva ad afferrare
allungando il braccio in tutte le direzioni;
questo permise alla NASA di individuare
il perimetro all'interno del quale dovevano
essere posti i comandi e i pulsanti che
dovevano essere utilizzati dall'astronauta
legato al sedile in fase di decollo e durante
le manovre.

Per questa scultura Cerqueira Leite rimette
in scena lo studio della NASA sull'area
di allungamento del braccio attraverso un
grande stampo in argilla, segnato dalle linee
delle sue dita mentre rimaneva seduta su un
sedile come quello dello Space Shuttle. La
scultura sferica che ne risulta non mostra
solo l'estensione del braccio dell'artista, ma
ridefinisce anche i confini e la forma del suo
corpo in azione.

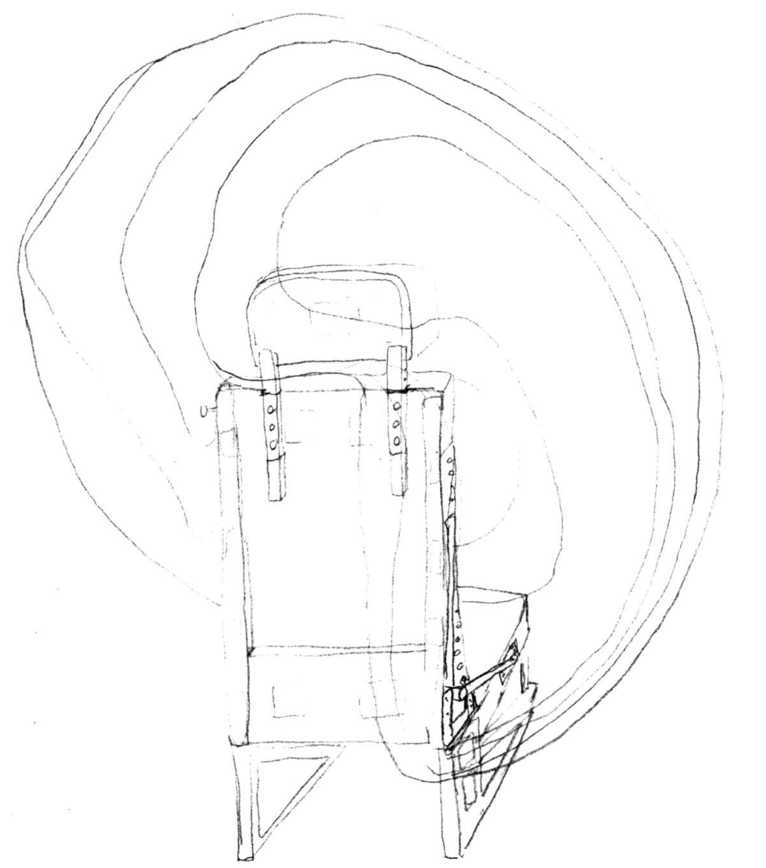

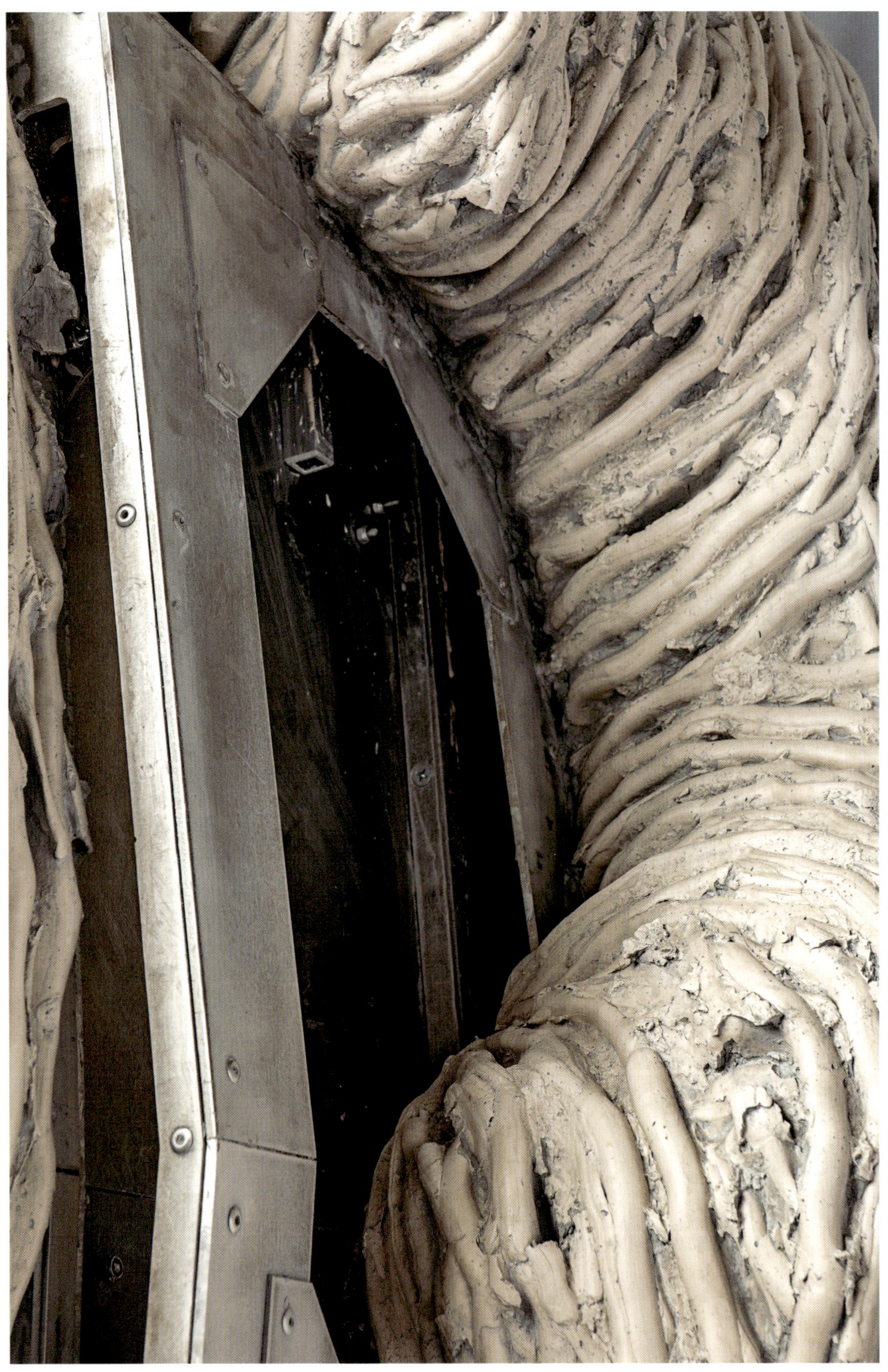

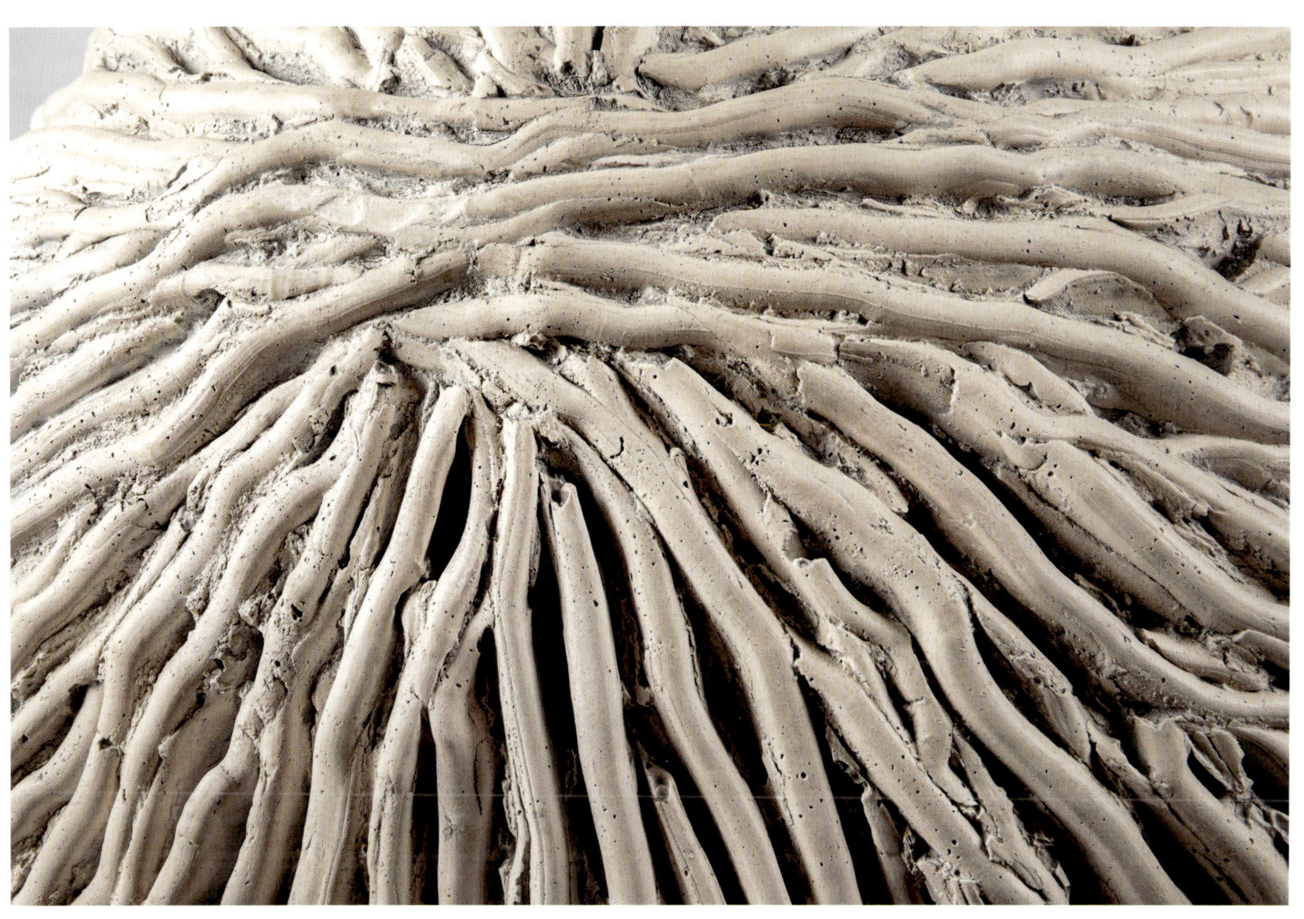

Species-Specific_005
2019
3D printed PLA, supports.

The term 'fight or flight' is commonly used
to describe a broad range of responses
that humans produce when under threat.
Although the kinds of responses that
we present as defensive behavior vary
according to variables, such as the ability
to defend one's self, ambiguity, threat, or
proximity of threat, these behaviors can
be described as species-specific: Humans
respond in specific ways, that are different
to how birds or horses respond to threat.
The calchi excavated in Pompeii are
mostly found in a crouched position with
their arms raised in what appears to be a
defensive response. In fact, most of the
inhabitants of Pompeii who were preserved
in ash were long dead before assuming this
position, which is a result of exposure to
the heat of the largest eruption of Vesuvius
in 79 AD.

This artwork was 3D printed by Fonderia
Nolana, near Naples, and was produced
from a 3D motion capture video of New
York-based dancer Meredith Glisson
performing a defense response to an
oncoming threat. Her movements were
captured in 120 frames per second of video
from a 360 degree camera array. What you
see here is approximately one second of
motion that has been sculpted to reveal the
nesting of her positions in time.

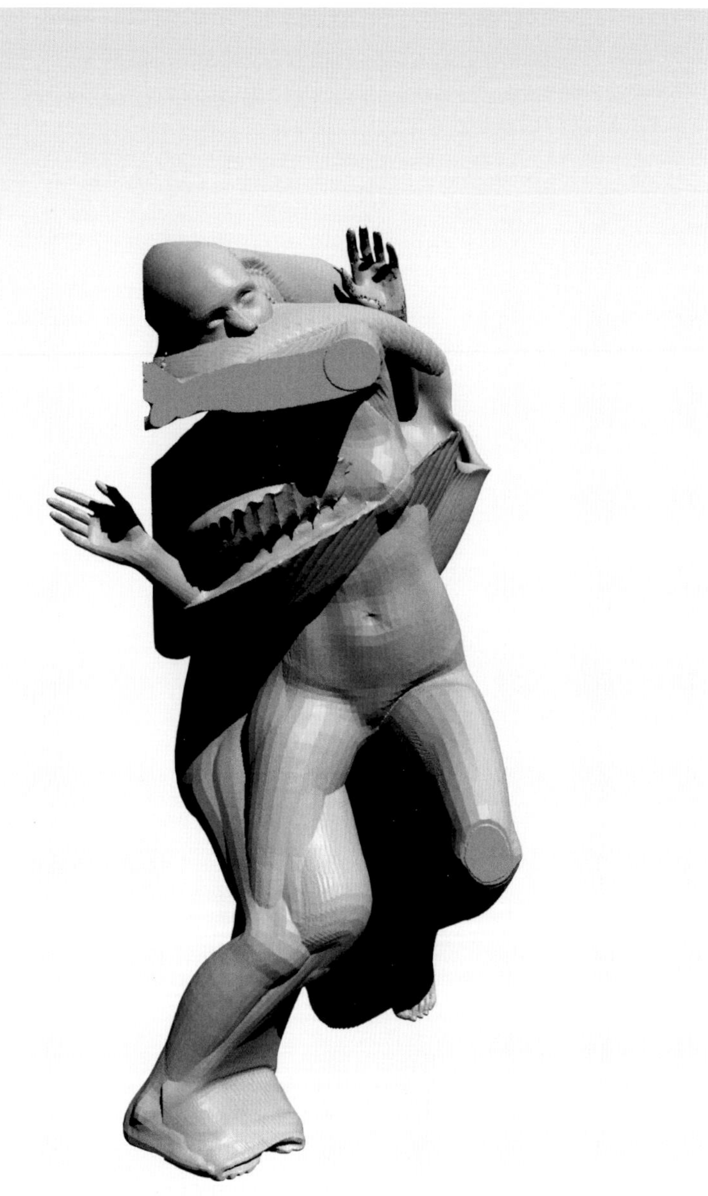

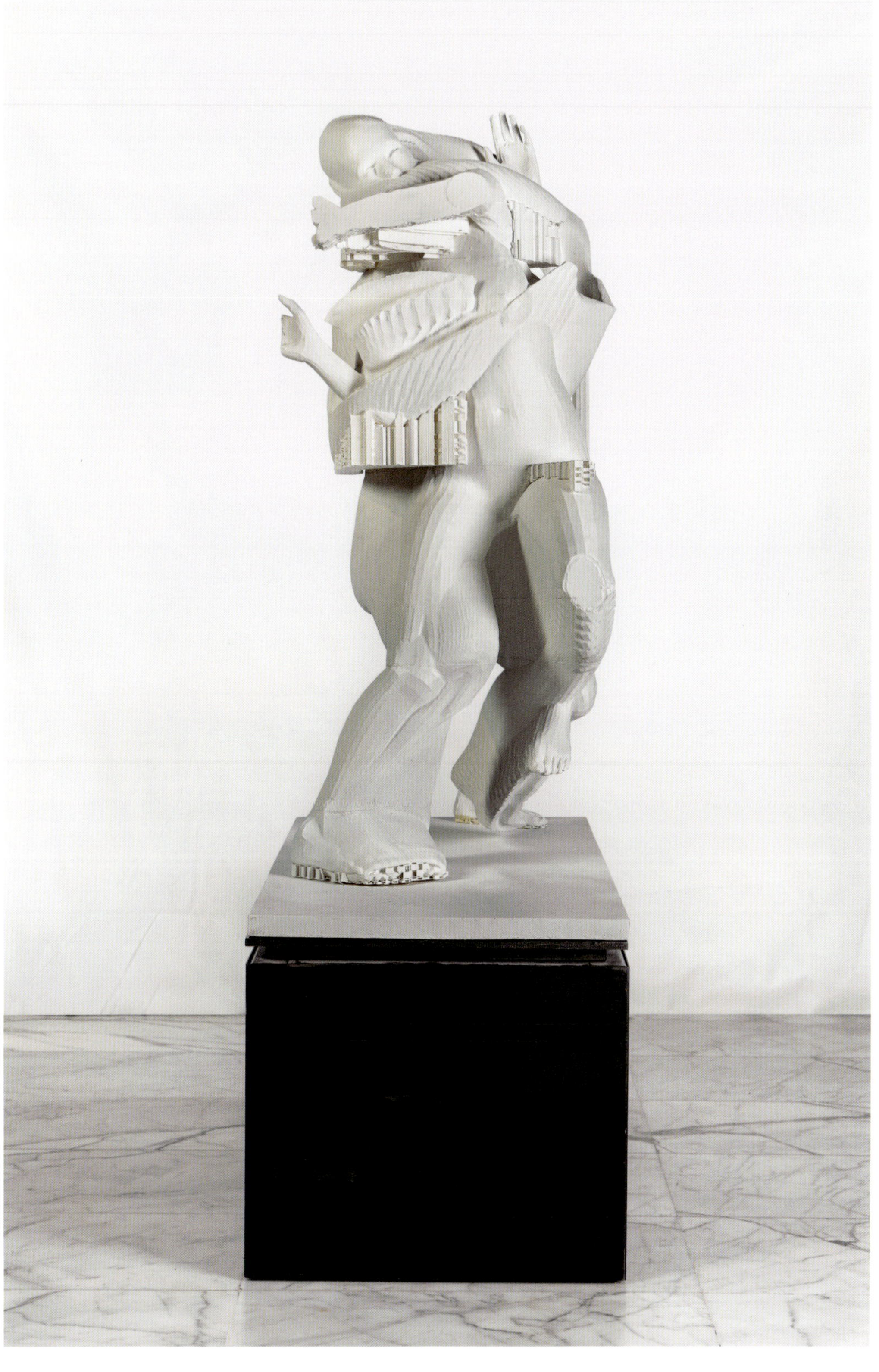

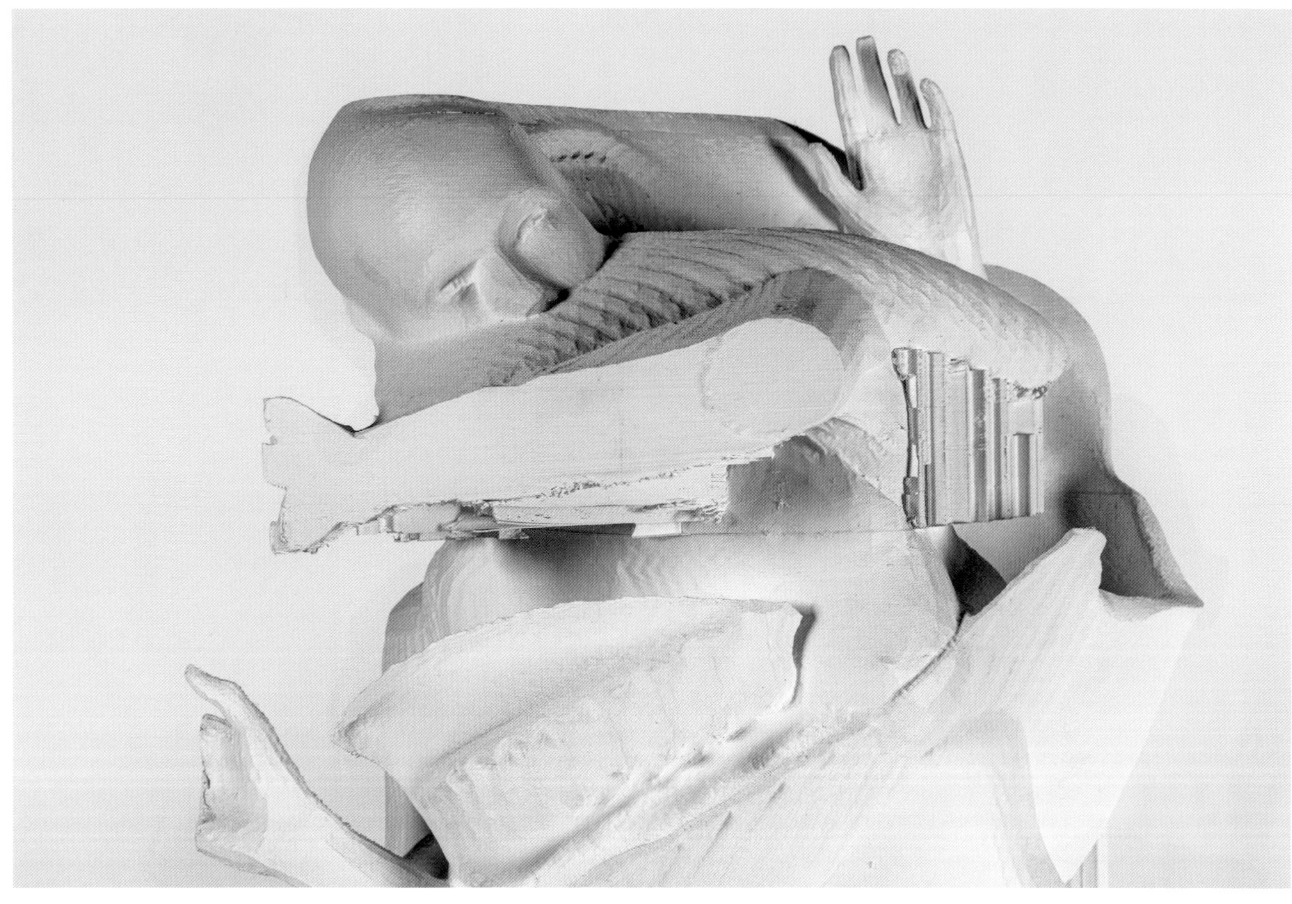

Specie-specifico_005
2019
PLA stampato in 3D, supporti.

Il termine "fight or flight" è usato in psicologia per definire un ampio raggio di reazioni dell'uomo quando si trova in pericolo. Sebbene la tipologia di risposte che interpretiamo come comportamento difensivo cambino a seconda di diverse variabili, come l'abilità di difendersi, ambiguità, vicinanza del pericolo, questi comportamenti possono essere descritti come specie-specifici: gli umani reagiscono alla minaccia in maniera propria alla loro specie, diversa dal modo in cui, ad esempio, uccelli o cavalli rispondono.

I calchi estratti a Pompei sono stati ritrovati in una posizione accovacciata, con le braccia sollevate in quella che appare come una reazione difensiva. In realtà la maggior parte degli abitanti di Pompei coperti dalle ceneri erano deceduti molto prima di assumere questa posizione, che è il risultato dell'esposizione al calore emesso dalla grande eruzione del Vesuvio del 79 d.C.

L'opera è stata stampata in 3D presso Fonderia Nolana, vicino a Napoli, ed è stata prodotta a partire da un video in 3D motion capture realizzato a New York, in cui la ballerina Meredith Glisson inscena una serie di reazioni di difesa da un pericolo incombente. I suoi movimenti sono stati registrati in un video a 120 fotogrammi al secondo, con una videocamera a 360 gradi. Ciò che si vede qui è il risultato di circa un secondo di video, scolpito a rivelare le sue posizioni nel tempo.

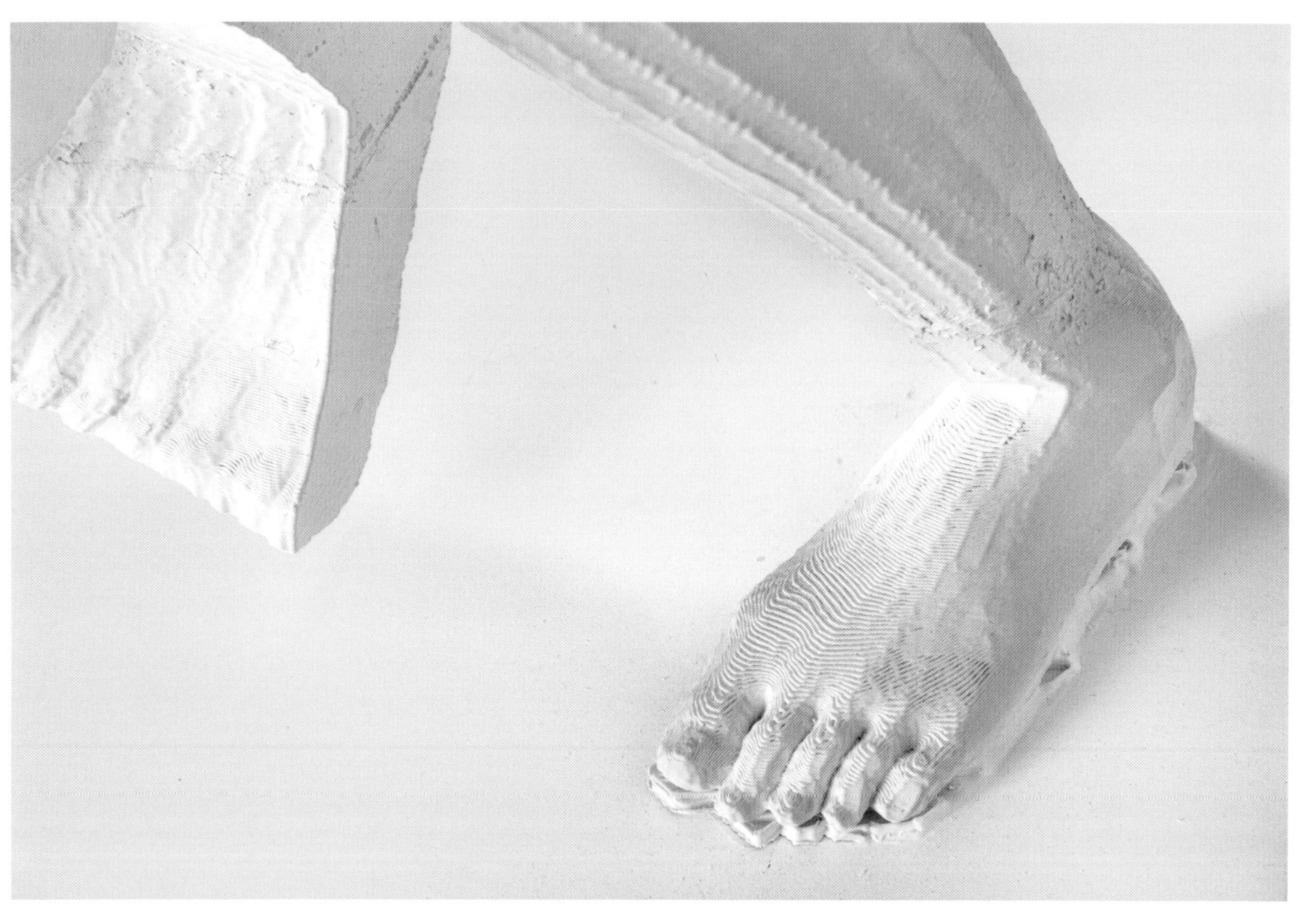

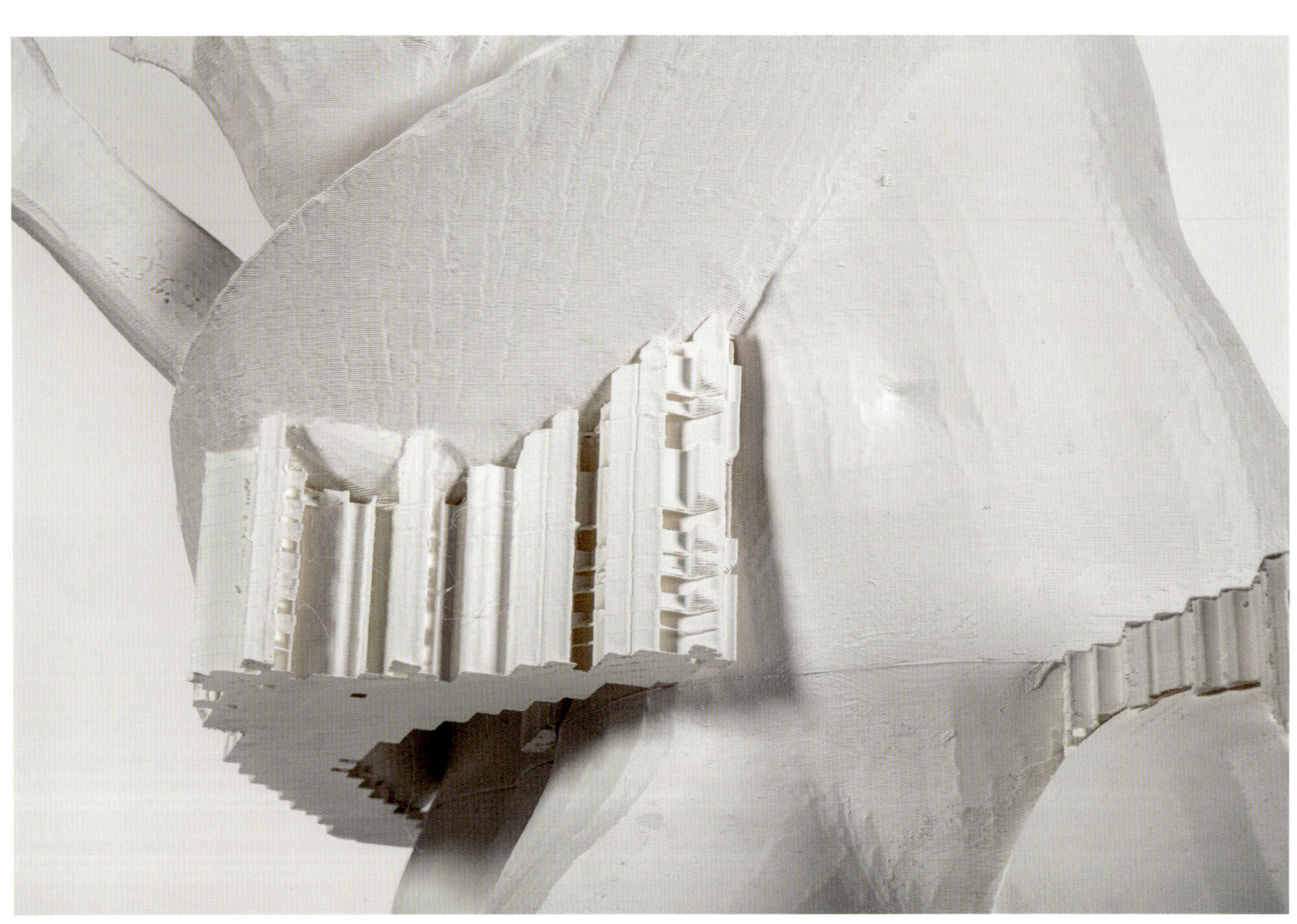

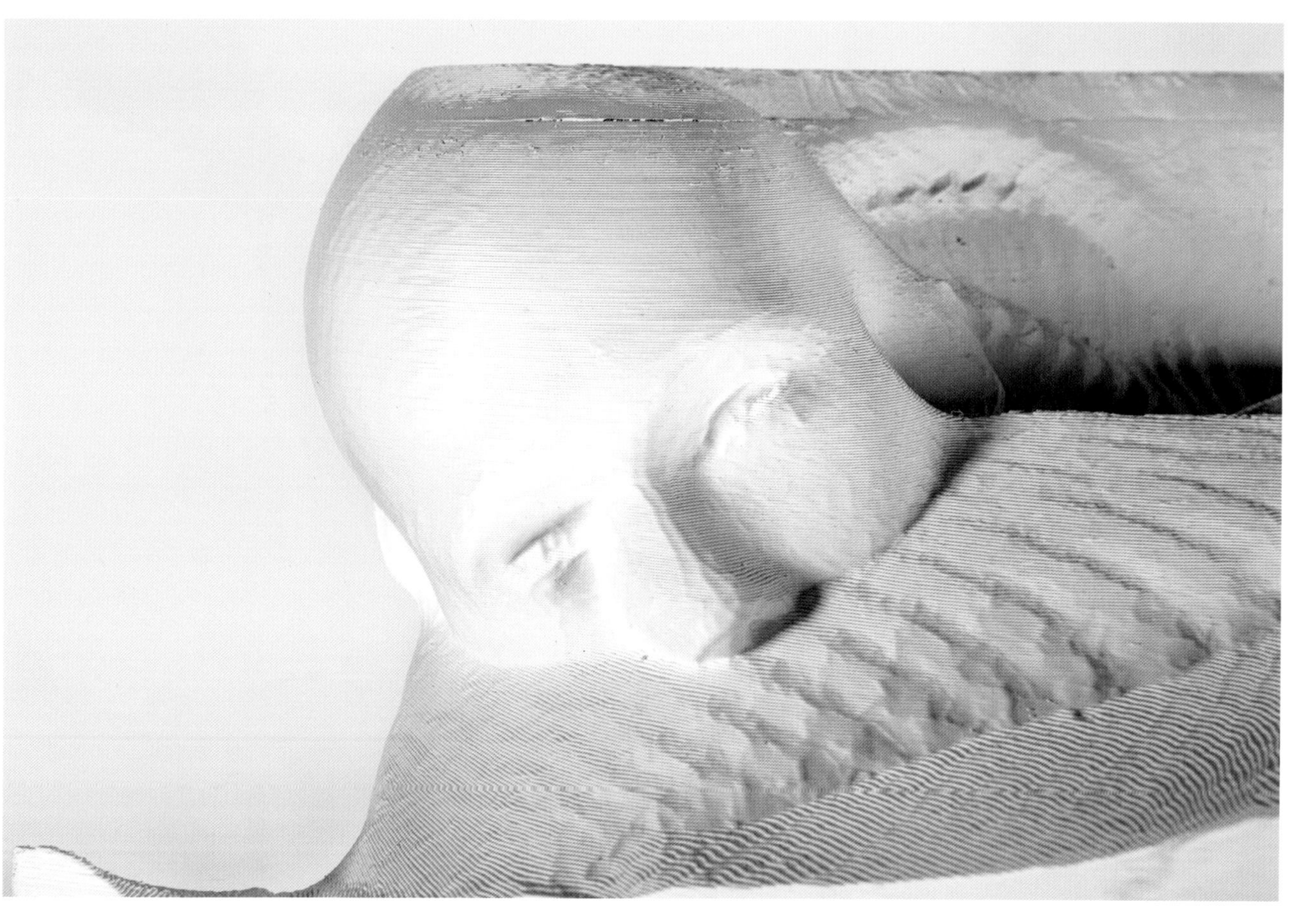

Calcify
2019
Aquaresin, Hydrocal, glass fiber, steel,
clay, pigment, glass, sand.

The famous calchi (the plaster cast bodies)
of Pompeii were first produced in 1863
by the director of excavations, Giuseppe
Fiorelli. Fiorelli was an innovator of the
field of archaeology. He invented what is
now known as the Fiorelli Process, where
holes found during archaeological digs, left
behind by decayed organic material, were
filled with plaster before their surroundings
were excavated. The plaster cast revealed
these holes as perfect molds of the organic
forms that previously gave them shape—
reproducing plants, animals, or, in the case
of the calchi, people.

In *Calcify* the artist reproduced her
body several times from molds using
negatives in clay and plaster. These
materials give different degrees of detail
and loss of information. Her position
is the familiar contracted pose of the
calchi, known to forensic scientists as
the pugilistic attitude—where the body
contracts posthumously into a boxer-like
pose following exposure to intense heat.
Fiorelli's calchi turned ancient Roman
bodies into fossils, time travelers and tragic
emblems of the power of nature. Similarly,
the limestone used in the construction of
Pompeii reveals fossils of an even more
ancient past: marine creatures trapped
in stone.

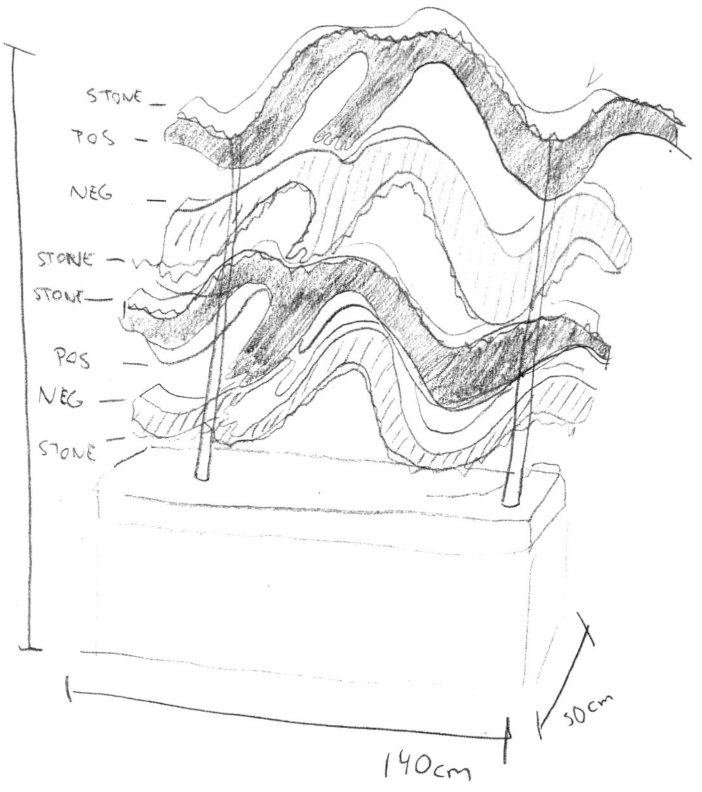

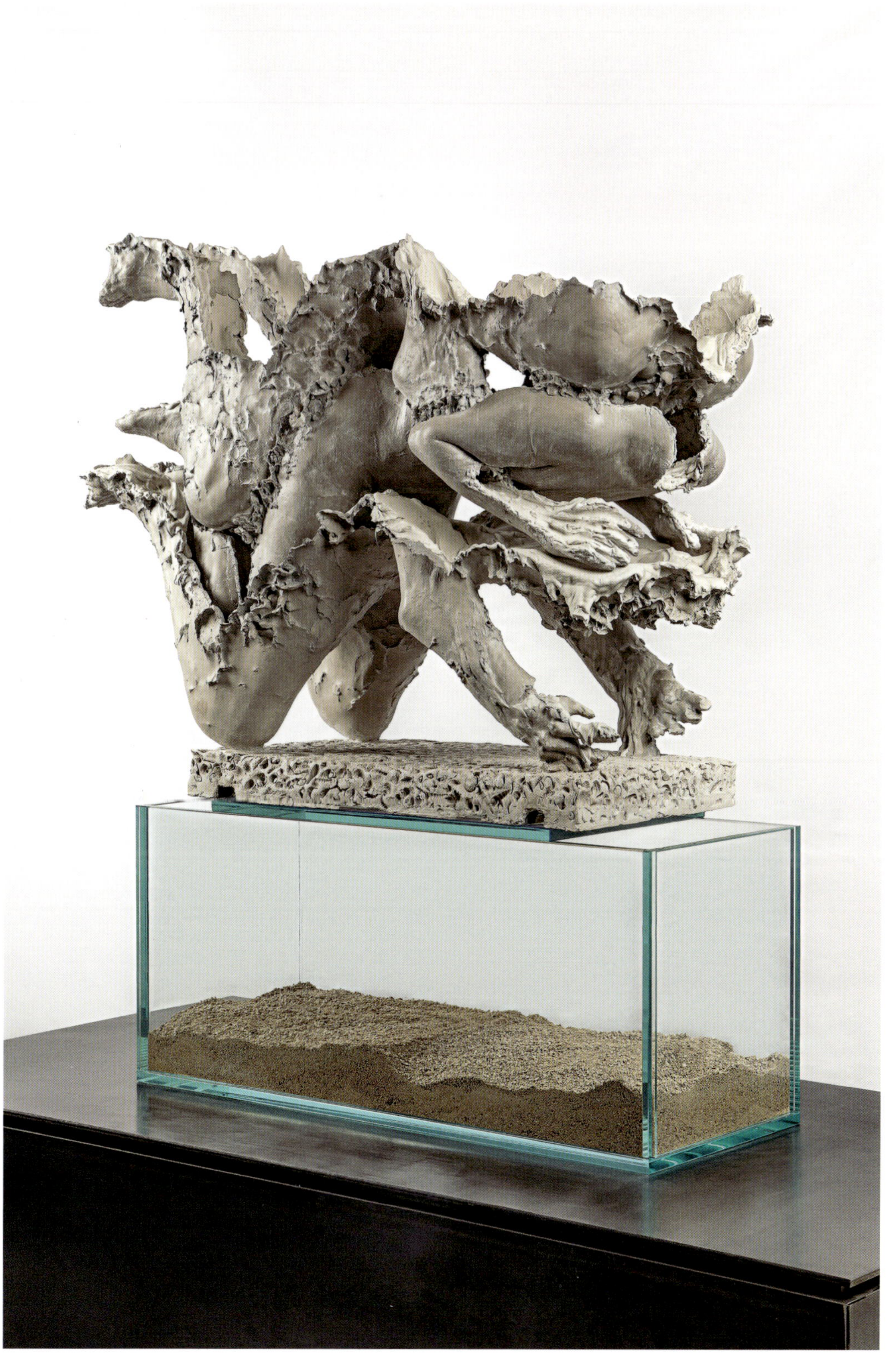

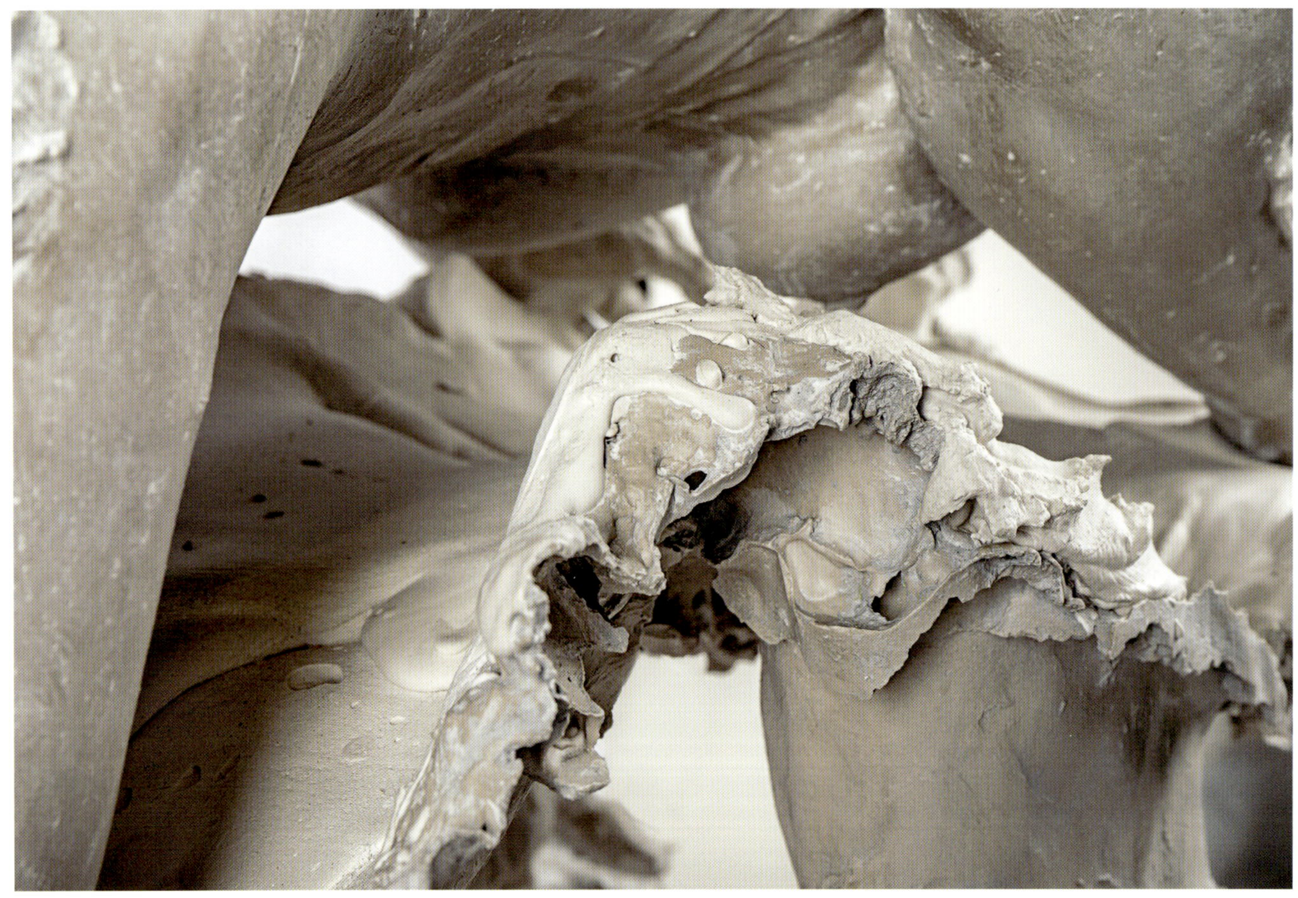

Calcificare
2019
Acquaresina, Hydrocal, fibra di vetro,
acciaio, argilla, pigmenti, vetro, sabbia.

I famosi calchi (gli stampi in gesso) di
Pompei hanno la loro origine a partire dal
1863 per opera del direttore degli scavi
del tempo, Giuseppe Fiorelli. Fiorelli fu
un innovatore nel campo dell'archeologia,
inventore di quella che è ora nota come la
Tecnica Fiorelli, che consisteva nel riempire
di gesso gli spazi vuoti che venivano
ritrovati nel terreno durante gli scavi,
residui di antico materiale organico ormai
deteriorato, prima di estrarli. I blocchi di
gesso divennero in questo modo gli stampi
perfetti delle forme che originariamente
occupavano questi spazi vuoti, e permisero
di riprodurre piante, animali o, nel caso dei
calchi, persone.

In *Calcify* l'artista riproduce il suo corpo
diverse volte utilizzando stampi creati con
negativi in argilla e gesso, materiali che
rendono i dettagli in maniera differente
e in cui alcuni particolari si perdono. La
postura del suo corpo rispecchia quella
contratta dei calchi, scientificamente nota
come posizione da pugile, nella quale il
corpo esposto a calore intenso si contrae
in una maniera che ricorda la guardia nel
pugilato. I calchi di Fiorelli hanno reso
gli antichi corpi dei Romani dei fossili,
viaggiatori nel tempo e tragici emblemi del
potere della natura. In maniera analoga, la
pietra calcarea utilizzata nella costruzione
di Pompei rivela fossili di un passato ancora
più antico: creature marine intrappolate
nella roccia.

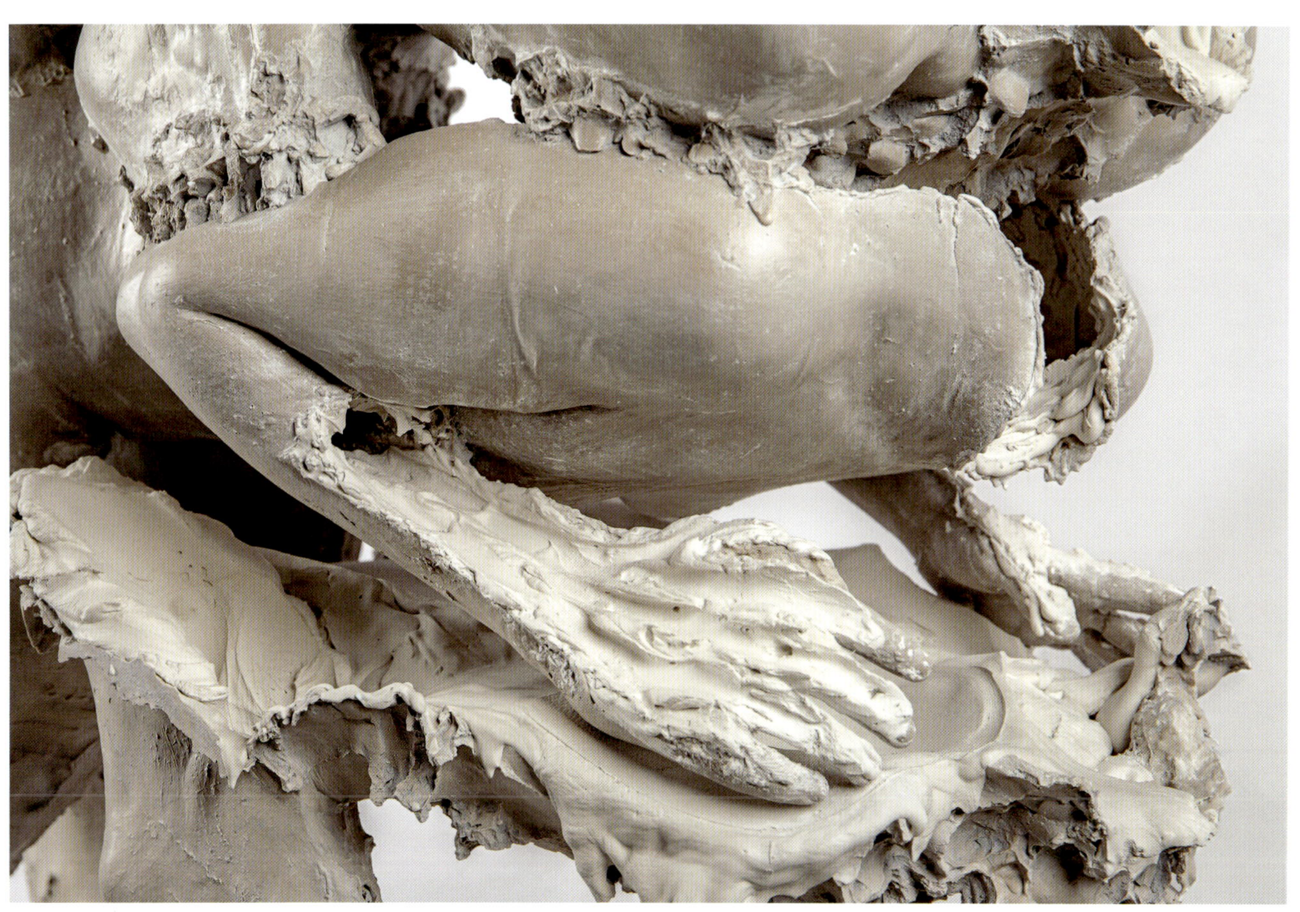

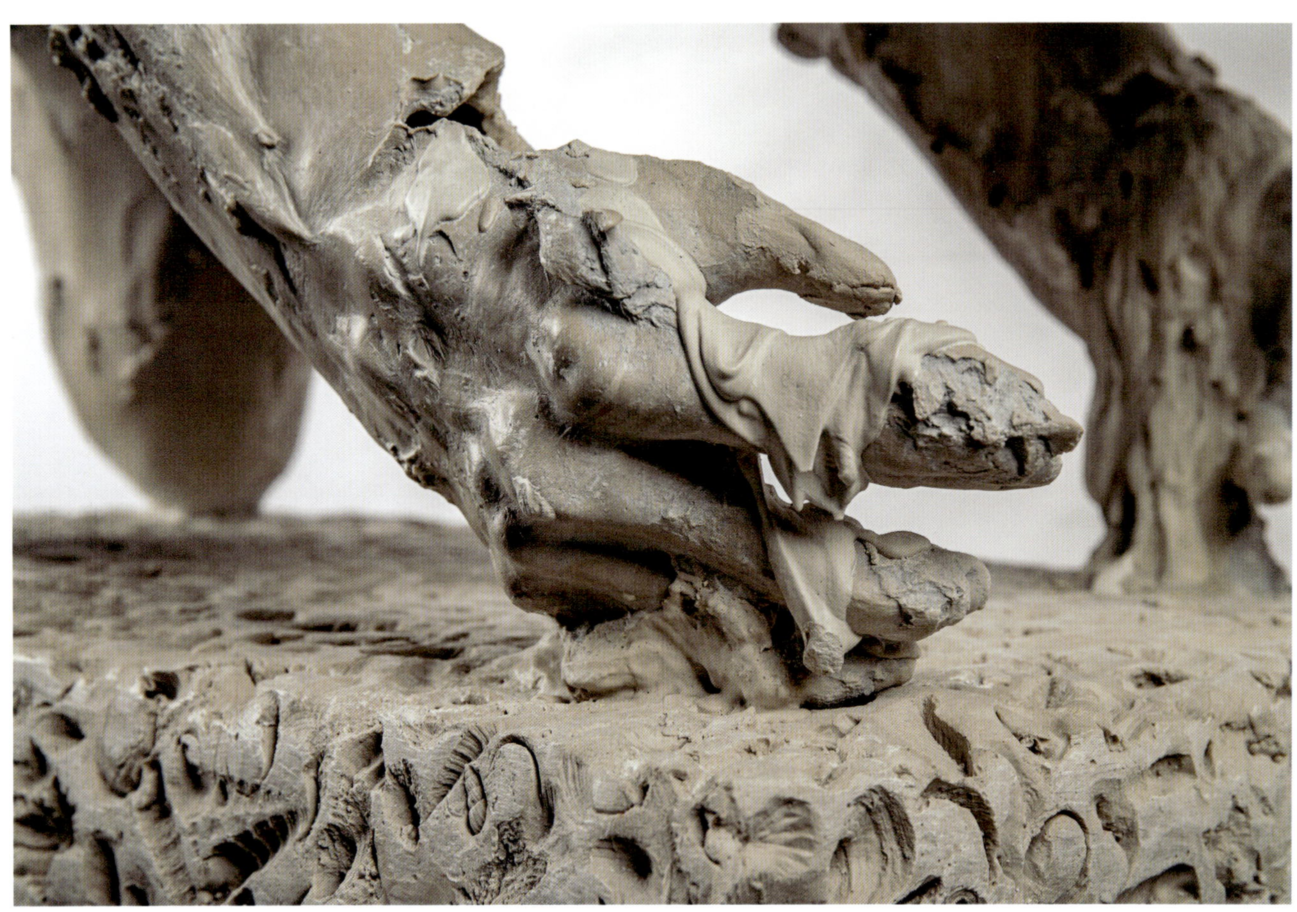

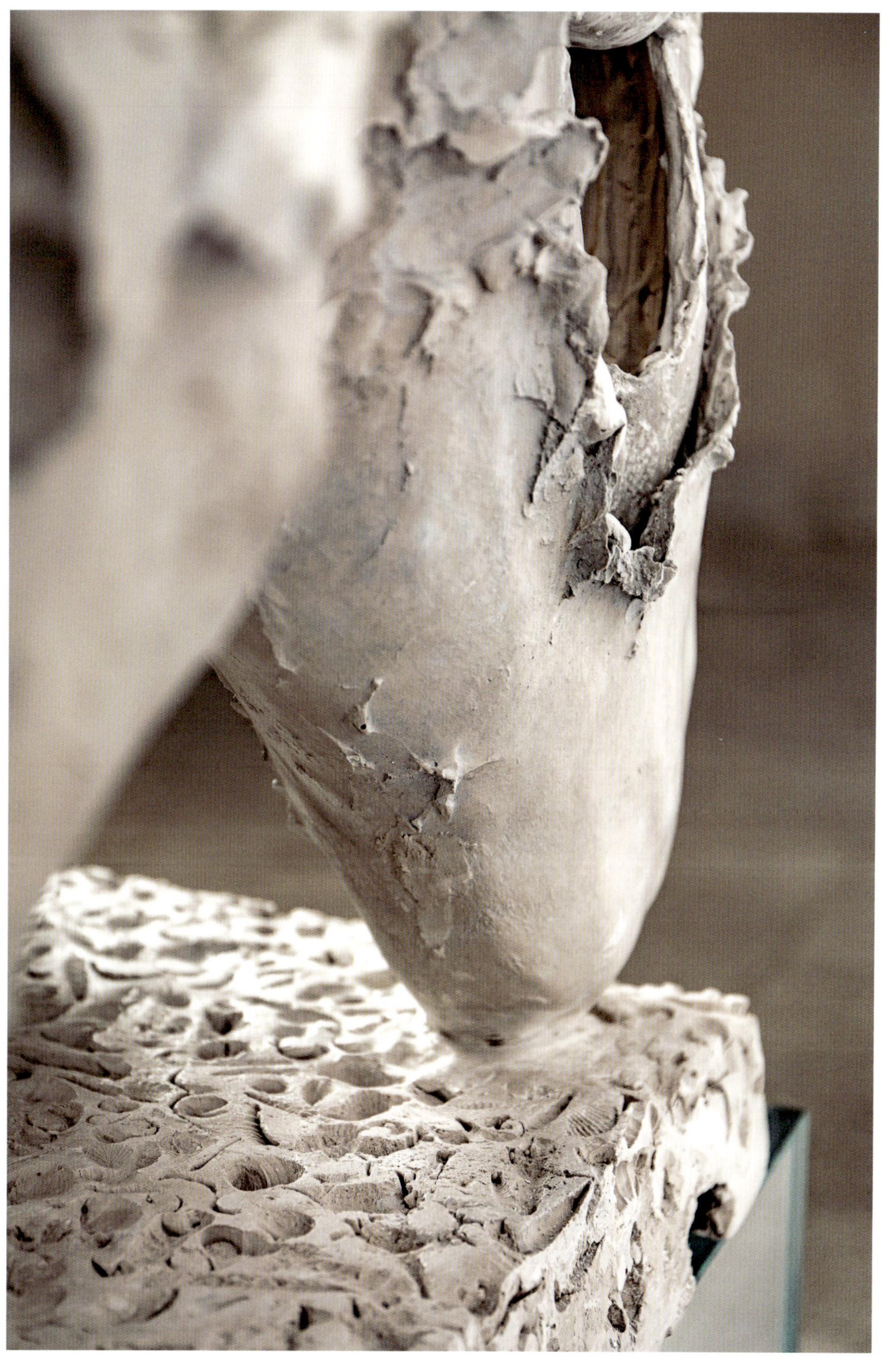

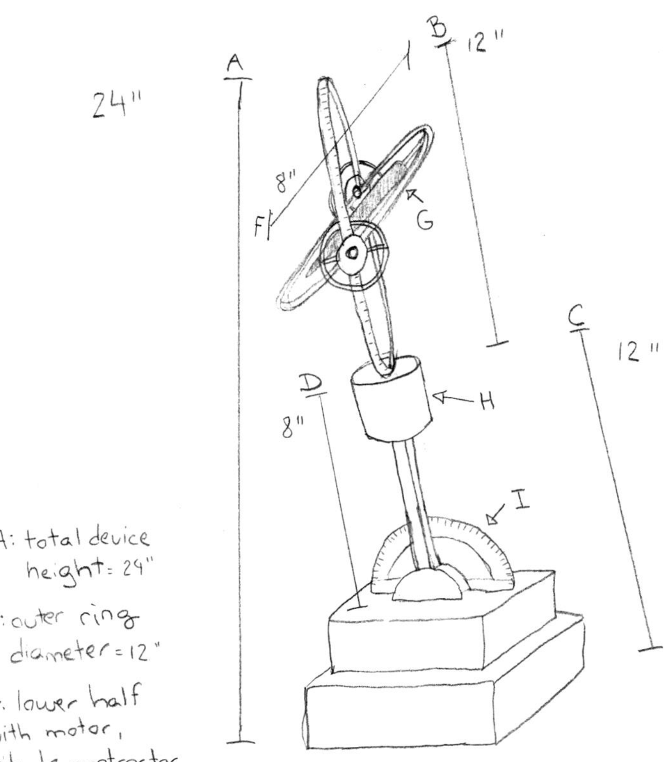

A: total device height: 24"

B: outer ring diameter = 12"

C: lower half with motor, latitude protractor and electronics = 12"

D: lower rod with motor + latitude protractor = 8"

E: width of electronic component box = 12"

F: inner ring diameter = 8"

G: stone point length = 4"

H: motor diameter estimated at 3" and length at 3"

I: latitude protractor estimate diameter = 6"

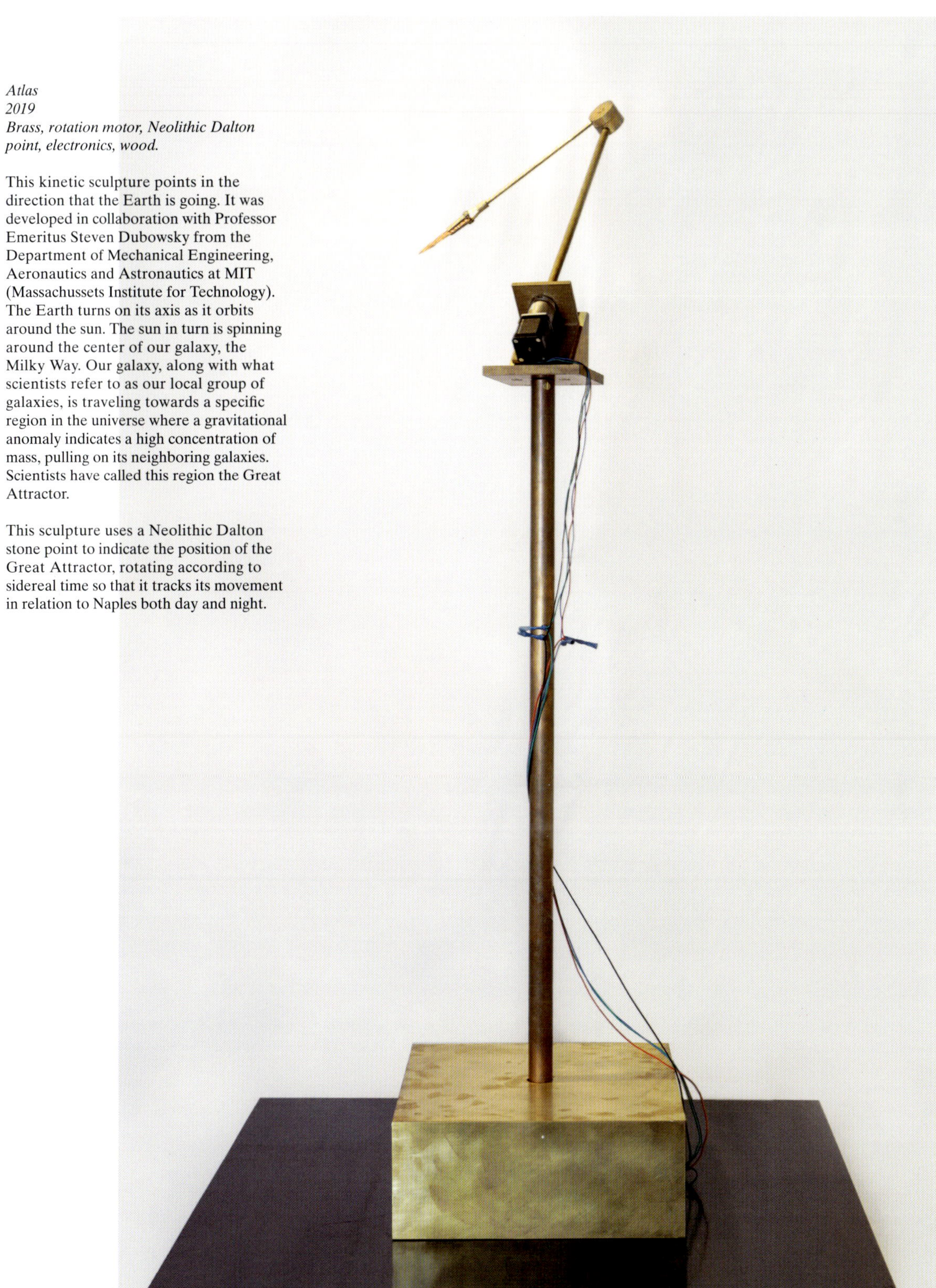

Atlas
2019
Brass, rotation motor, Neolithic Dalton
point, electronics, wood.

This kinetic sculpture points in the direction that the Earth is going. It was developed in collaboration with Professor Emeritus Steven Dubowsky from the Department of Mechanical Engineering, Aeronautics and Astronautics at MIT (Massachussets Institute for Technology). The Earth turns on its axis as it orbits around the sun. The sun in turn is spinning around the center of our galaxy, the Milky Way. Our galaxy, along with what scientists refer to as our local group of galaxies, is traveling towards a specific region in the universe where a gravitational anomaly indicates a high concentration of mass, pulling on its neighboring galaxies. Scientists have called this region the Great Attractor.

This sculpture uses a Neolithic Dalton stone point to indicate the position of the Great Attractor, rotating according to sidereal time so that it tracks its movement in relation to Naples both day and night.

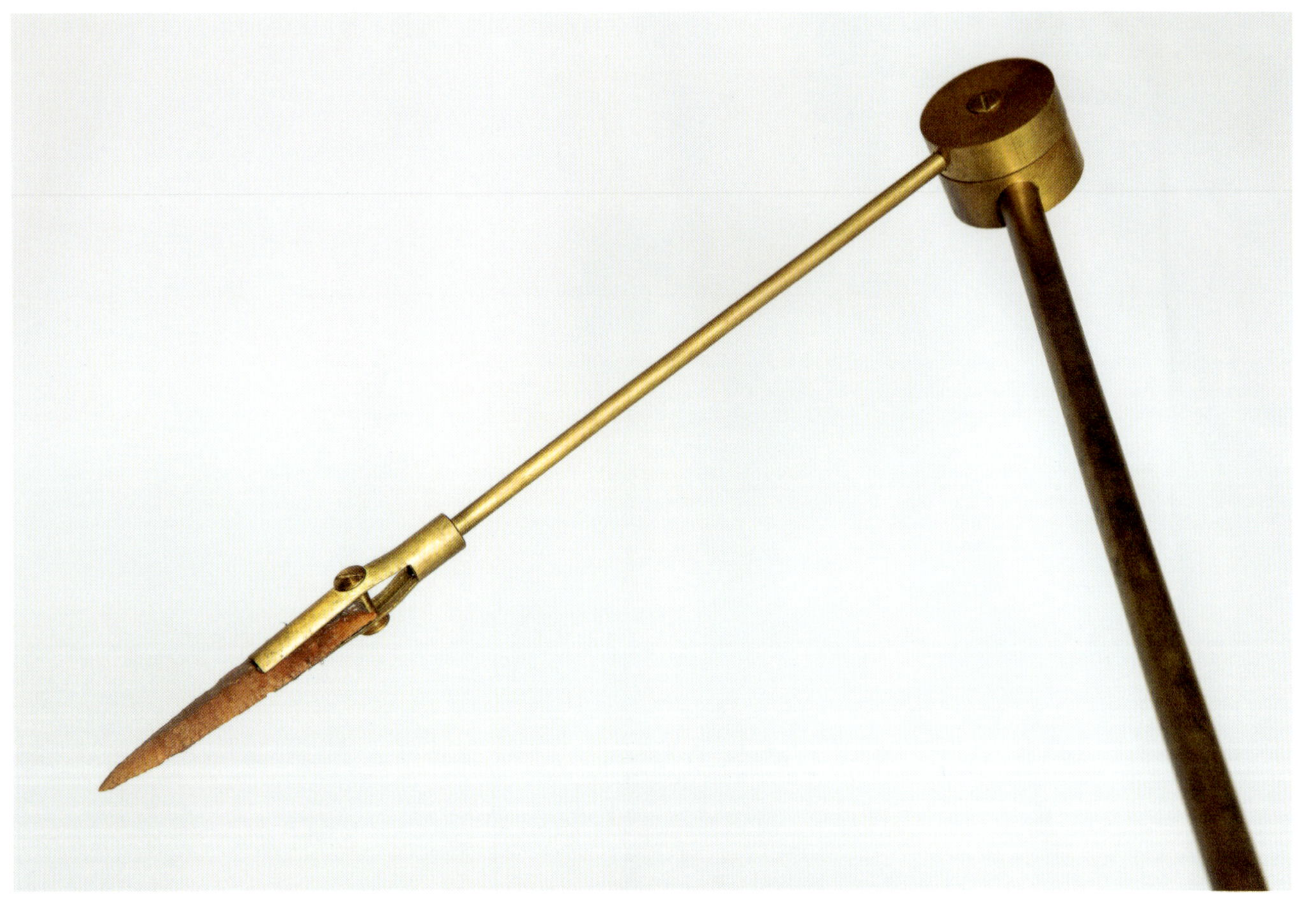

Atlante
2019
Ottone, motore rotante, punta di lancia
neolitica, componenti elettroniche, legno.

Questa scultura cinetica punta sempre
verso la direzione in cui la Terra si sta
muovendo, ed è stata sviluppata in
collaborazione con il Professor Steven
Dubowsky del Department of Mechanical
Engineering, Aeronautics and Astronautics
del MIT (Massachussets Institute for
Technology).

La Terra ruota attorno al suo asse e orbita
attorno al Sole, il quale a sua volta ruota
attorno al centro della nostra galassia,
la Via Lattea. Quest'ultima, assieme al
gruppo di galassie di cui fa parte, viaggia
verso una specifica regione dell'universo
dove un'anomalia gravitazionale indica una
grande concentrazione di massa che attrae
le galassie vicine. Gli scienziati hanno
denominato questa regione "il Grande
Attrattore". Questa scultura utilizza una
pietra neolitica per indicare la posizione
del Grande Attrattore, e ruota secondo il
tempo siderale in modo da tracciare il suo
movimento in relazione a Napoli di giorno
e di notte.

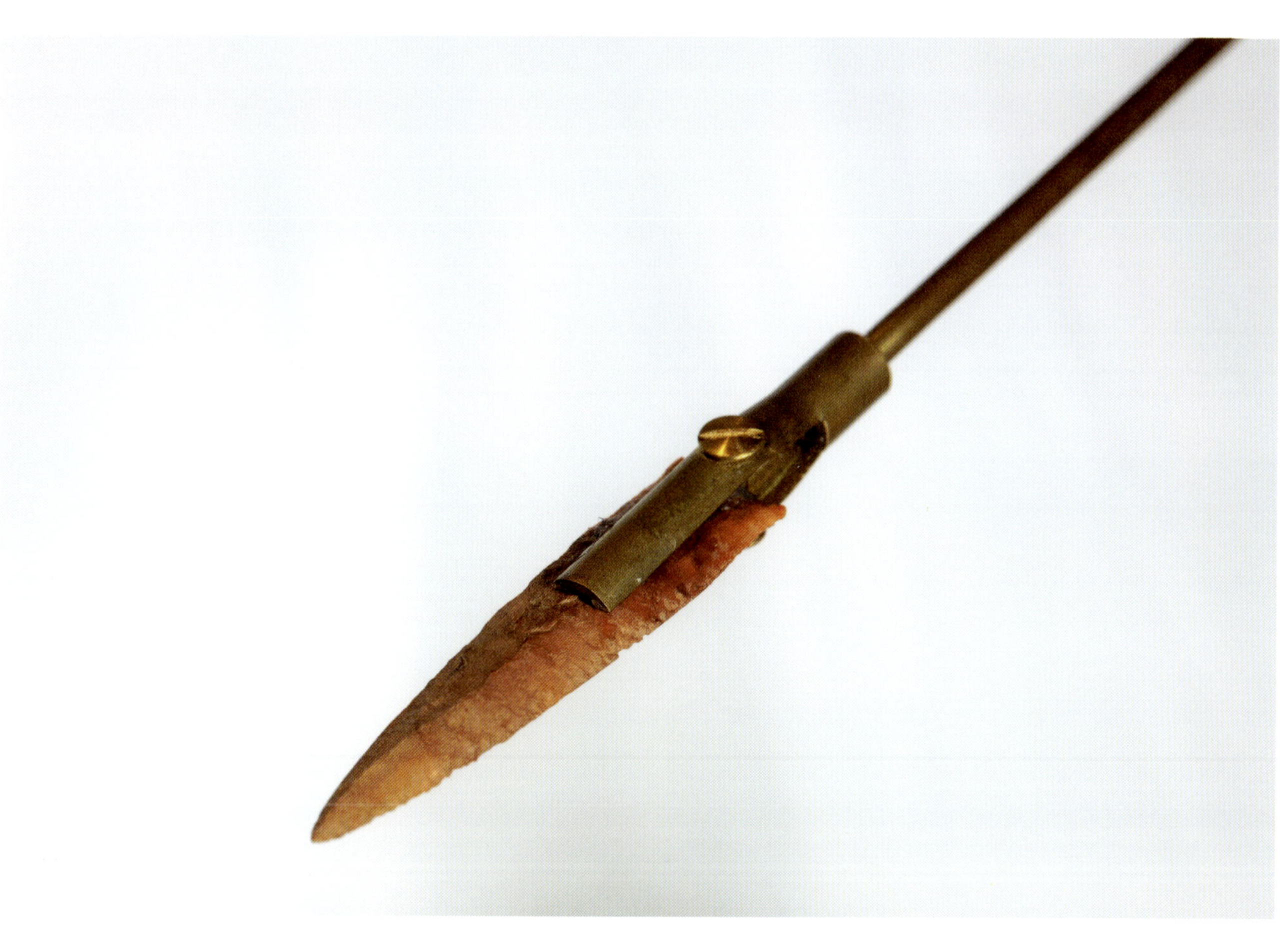

Contraction 1 & 2
2019
Plaster, steel.

This pair of sculptures reveal a body
fragmented into its articulations. Wrists,
ankles, knees, elbows, shoulders and hips
are disjointedly stacked as absence, as
plaster totems.

For this exhibition Cerqueira Leite has
focused on the repetition of the human
body in a contracted pose that seems to
repeat itself in different contexts and
with different intentions. The pose is
joined across its repetitions through
the persistence of the human anatomy,
which brings the body repeatedly into
this position despite changes in culture,
technology, and time.

Here, the artist stacks the body's
articulations, producing curved tunnels
similar to escaping air from porous stone,
or the gaps left by the bodies that became
the calchi—absences that allow us to see
through the sculpture.

Queste due sculture rivelano un corpo frammentato nelle sue articolazioni. Polsi, caviglie, ginocchia, gomiti, spalle e fianchi sono accatastati in maniera sconnessa, assenti, come totem di gesso.

Per la mostra Cerqueira Leite si è concentrata sulla ripetizione del corpo umano in una posizione contratta che sembra ripresentarsi in diversi contesti e con intenzioni differenti. Questa postura è unita nelle sue varie ripetizioni attraverso la continuità dell'anatomia umana, che porta il corpo ad assumere ricorrentemente la posizione nonostante i cambiamenti culturali, tecnologici e cronologici.

In questo caso l'artista impila le articolazioni del corpo tra di loro, producendo una serie di aperture ricurve simili a quelle che si ritrovano nella pietra spugnosa, o agli spazi vuoti lasciati nel terreno dai corpi poi diventati i calchi, assenze che ci permettono di vedere attraverso la scultura.

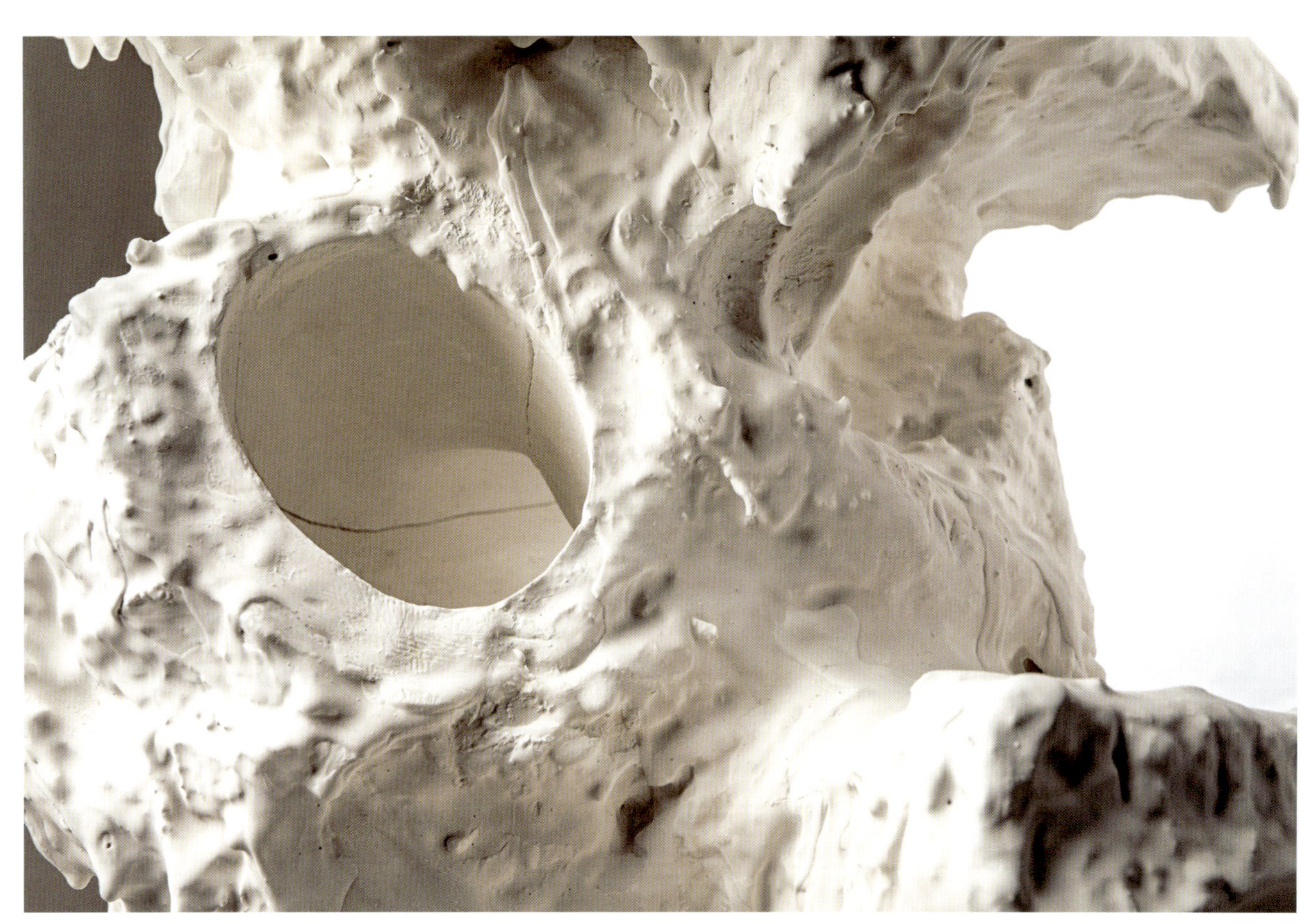

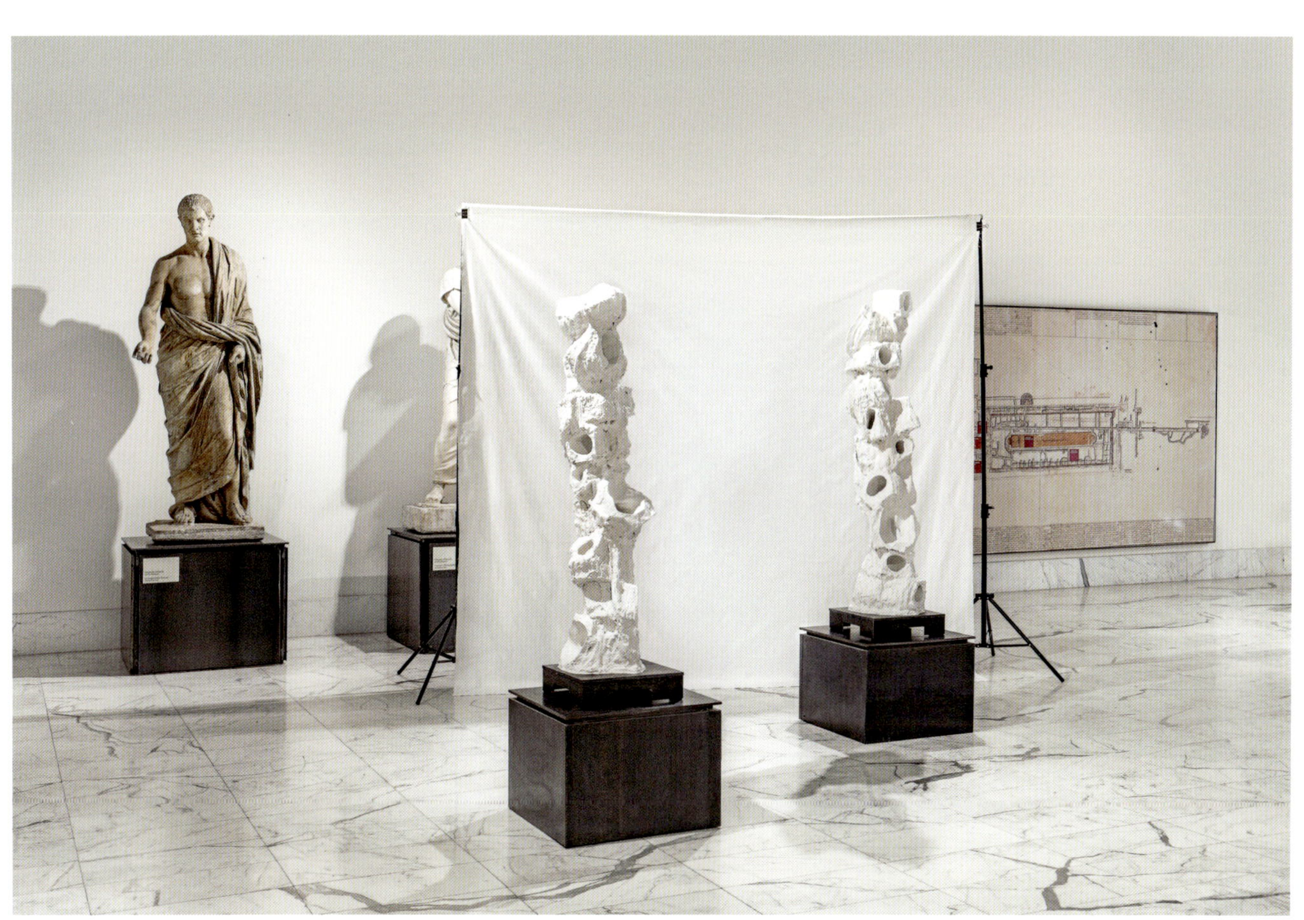

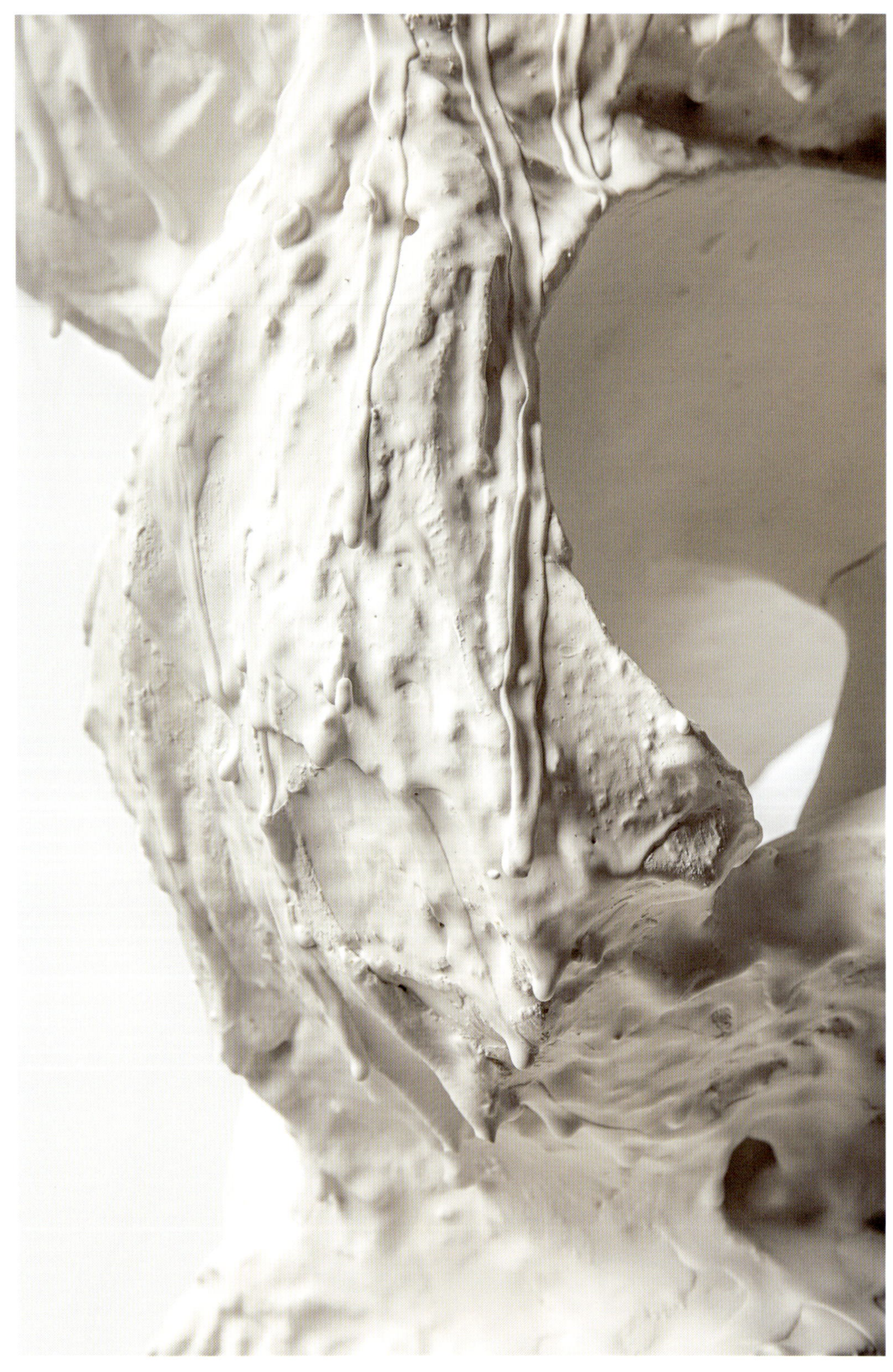

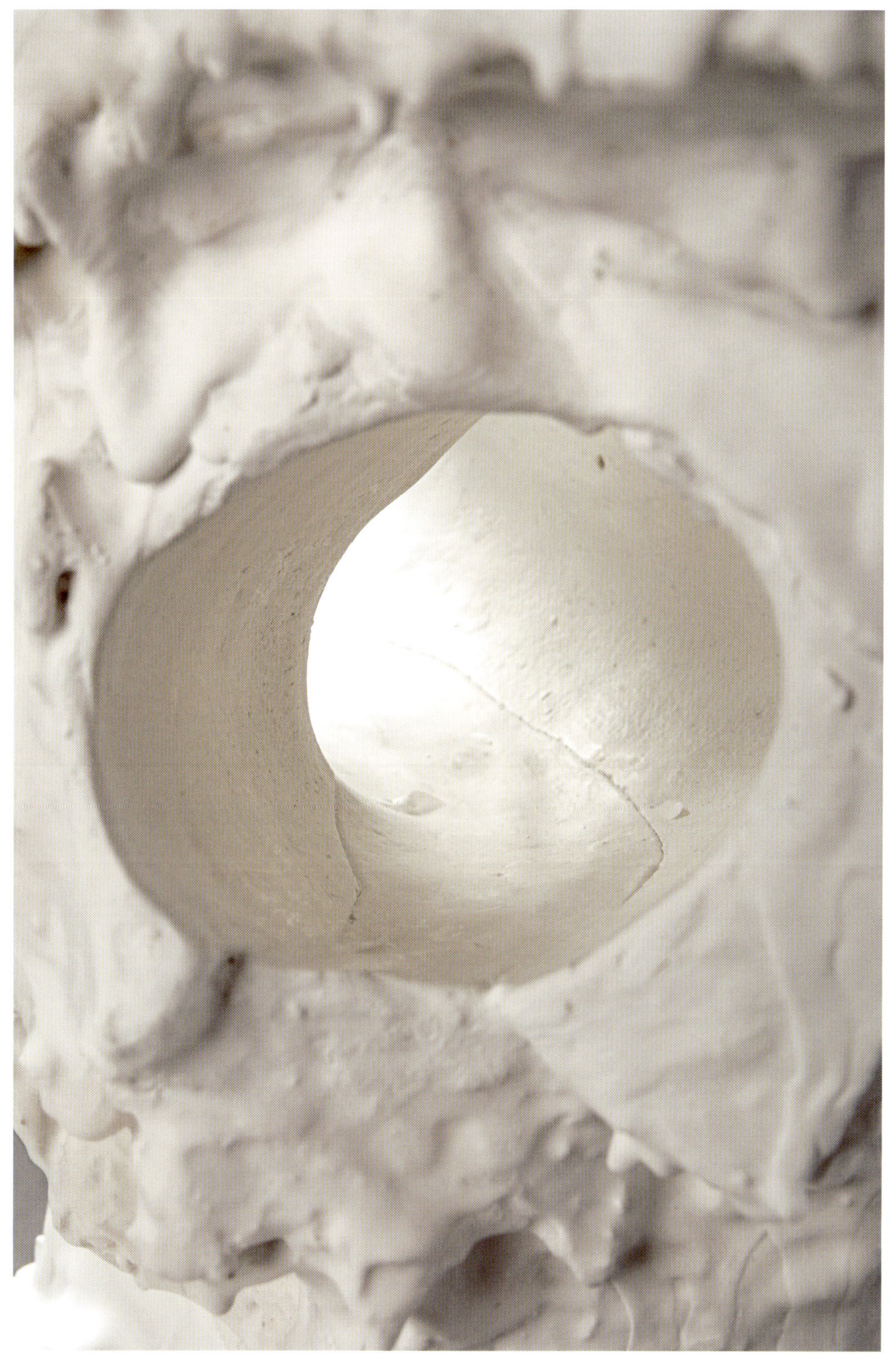

Contraction 3
2019
Plaster, steel.

This sculpture reveals a body fragmented
into its articulations. Wrists, ankles,
knees, elbows, shoulders and hips are
disjointedly stacked in absence as a plaster
wall—similarly to how several ancient
architectural elements are supported by
scaffolding and steel in Pompeii.

For this exhibition Cerqueira Leite has
focused on the repetition of the human
body in a contracted pose that seems to
repeat itself in different contexts and
with different intentions. The pose is
joined across its repetitions through
the persistence of the human anatomy,
as it brings the body repeatedly into
this position despite changes in culture,
technology, and time.

Here the artist stacks the body's
articulations, producing curved tunnels
similar to escaping air producing porous
stone, or the gaps left by the bodies that
became the calchi, and absences that allow
us to see through the sculpture.

Contrazione 3
2019
Gesso, alluminio.

Questa scultura rivela un corpo
frammentato nelle sue articolazioni. Polsi,
caviglie, ginocchia, gomiti, spalle e fianchi
sono accatastati in maniera sconnessa
a formare un muro di gesso, in maniera
simile alle impalcature che sorreggono
diversi antichi elementi architettonici a
Pompei.

Per la mostra Cerqueira Leite si è
concentrata sulla ripetizione del corpo
umano in una posizione contratta che
sembra ripresentarsi in diversi contesti e
con intenzioni differenti. Questa postura è
unita nelle sue varie ripetizioni attraverso
la continuità dell'anatomia umana, che
porta il corpo ad assumere ricorrentemente
la posizione nonostante i cambiamenti
culturali, tecnologici e cronologici.

In questo caso l'artista impila le
articolazioni del corpo tra di loro,
producendo una serie di aperture ricurve
simili a quelle che si ritrovano nella pietra
spugnosa, o agli spazi vuoti lasciati nel
terreno dai corpi poi diventati i calchi,
assenze che ci permettono di vedere
attraverso la scultura.

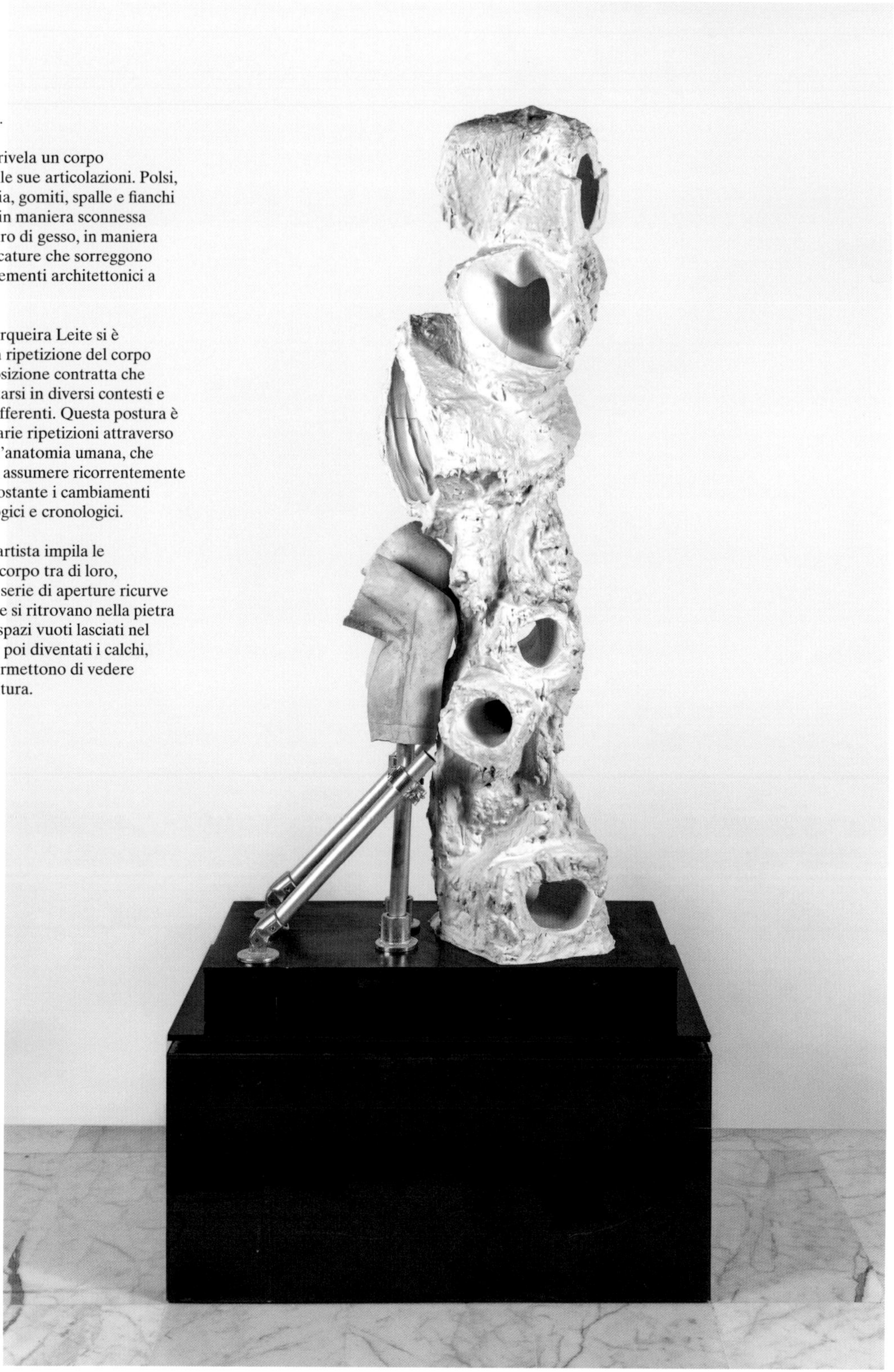

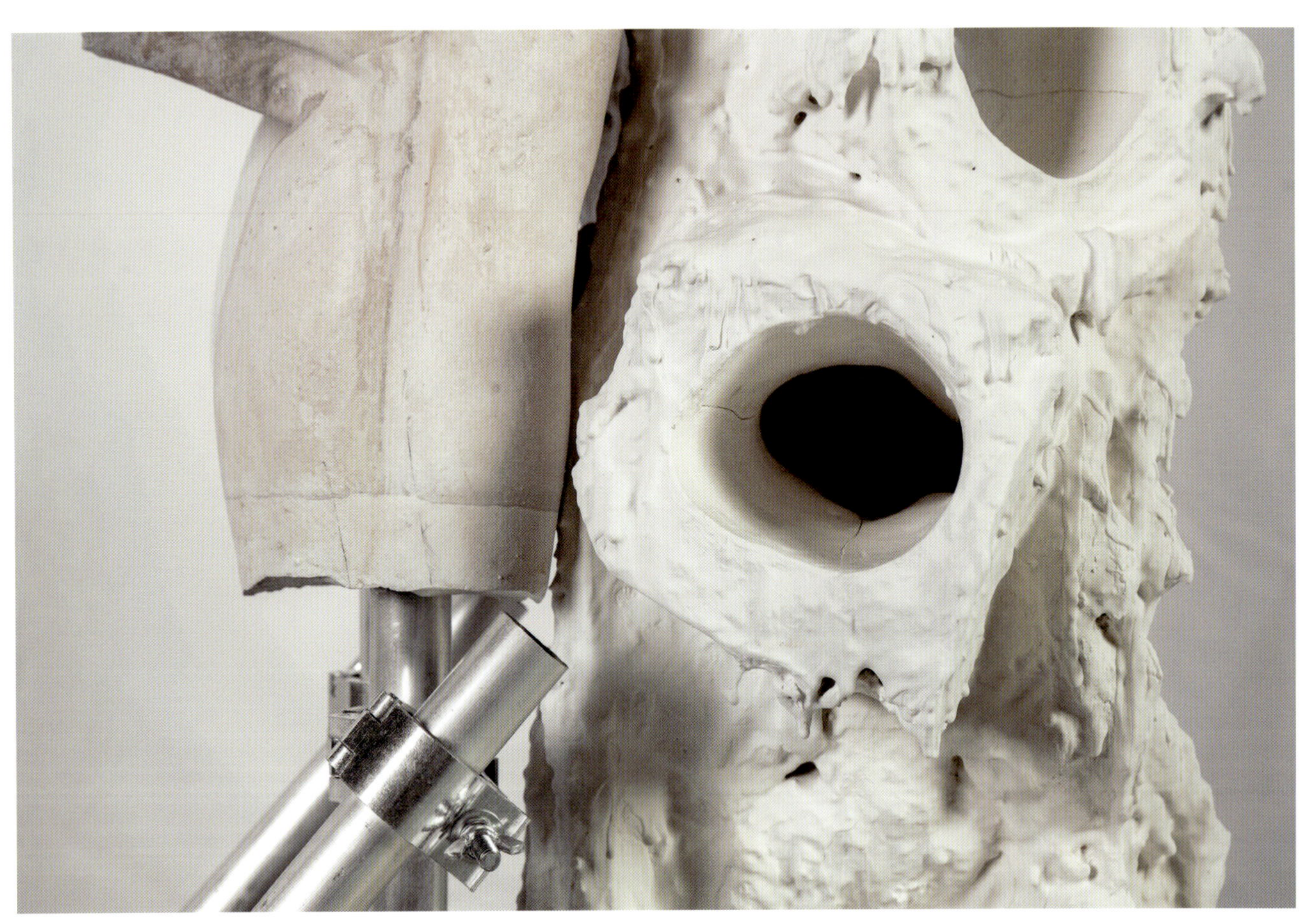

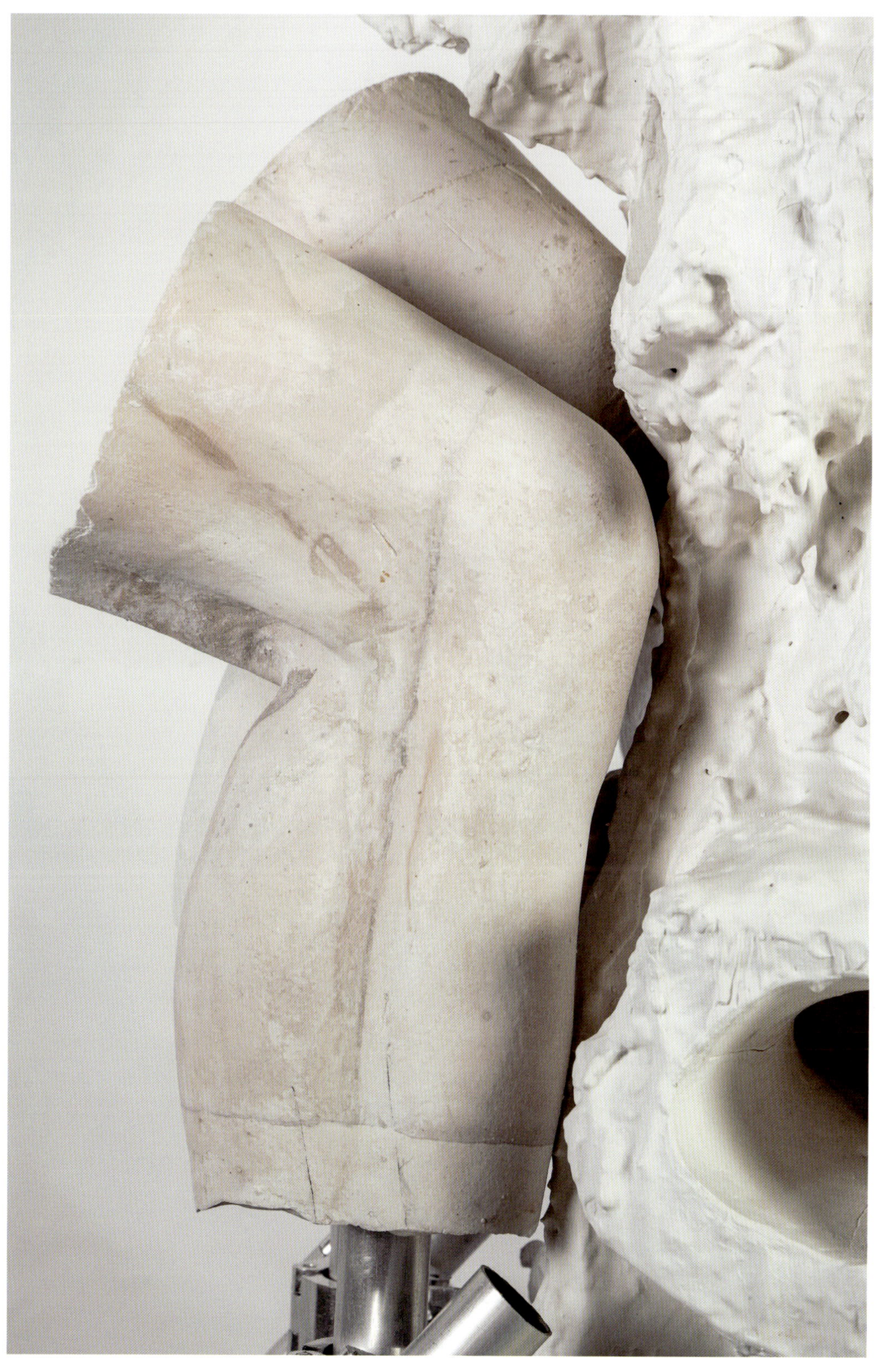

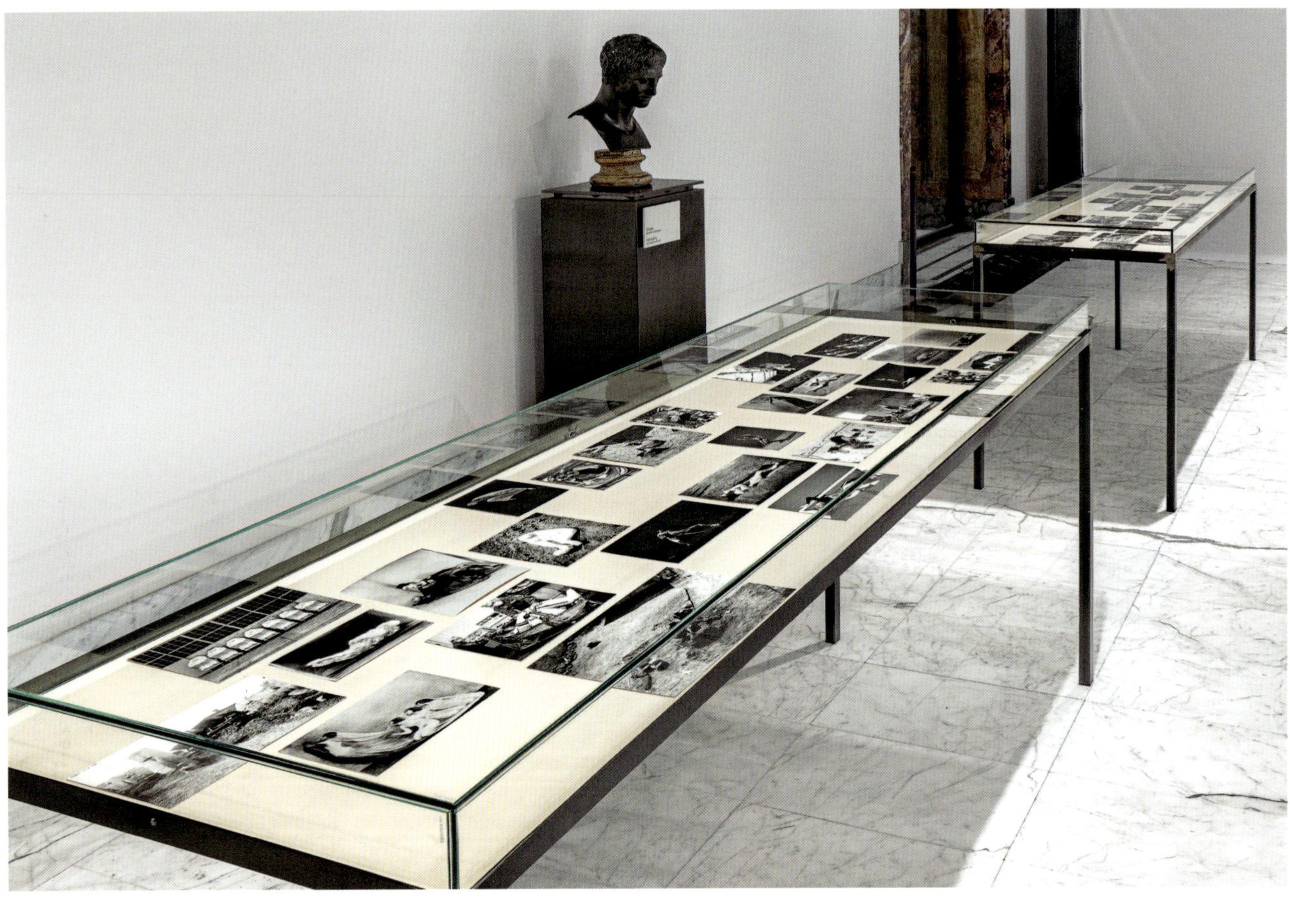

The photographs in these display cases were selected from the archives of the Archaeological Site of Pompeii, NASA, the Library of Congress in Washington DC, and the New York Public Library. The three contexts referenced in this exhibition are historical moments in which long periods of intense work led to breakthroughs in archaeology, dance and space exploration. These are moments in which humanity redefined its history.

In the first display case photographs show the uncanny re-occurrence of a contracted body pose see in the calchi excavated in Pompeii, whose bodies are in the 'pugilistic attitude'; astronauts in the 'neutral body posture,' or the natural posture of a humn body floating in zero gravity as described by NASA; and the 'contraction' as defined by the dancer and choreographer Martha Graham. Graham used the 'contraction' as an expression of intense emotion. Her dancers simultaneously collapsed and used their core muscles to pull their bodies into a compressed position.

In the second display case photographs show groups of dancers, engineers, astronauts, and archaeologists at work in images that self-consciously document collective labor, and the presentation of physical results.

Le fotografie raccolte in questa teca sono state selezionate dagli archivi fotografici del Sito Archeologico di Pompei, della NASA, della Library of Congress di Washington DC, e della New York Public Library. Tutti e tre i contesti che fanno da cornice a questa mostra sono momenti in cui lunghi periodi di intenso lavoro hanno portato a svolte metodologiche per l'archeologia, la danza e l'esplorazione dello spazio. Sono tutti momenti in cui l'umanità ha compiuto sforzi per ridefinire se stessa.

Nella prima teca le fotografie mostrano una specifica posizione del corpo umano, ritrovata nei calchi scavato a Pompei, detta "posizione da pugile"; astronauti nella postura standard assunta in ambiente

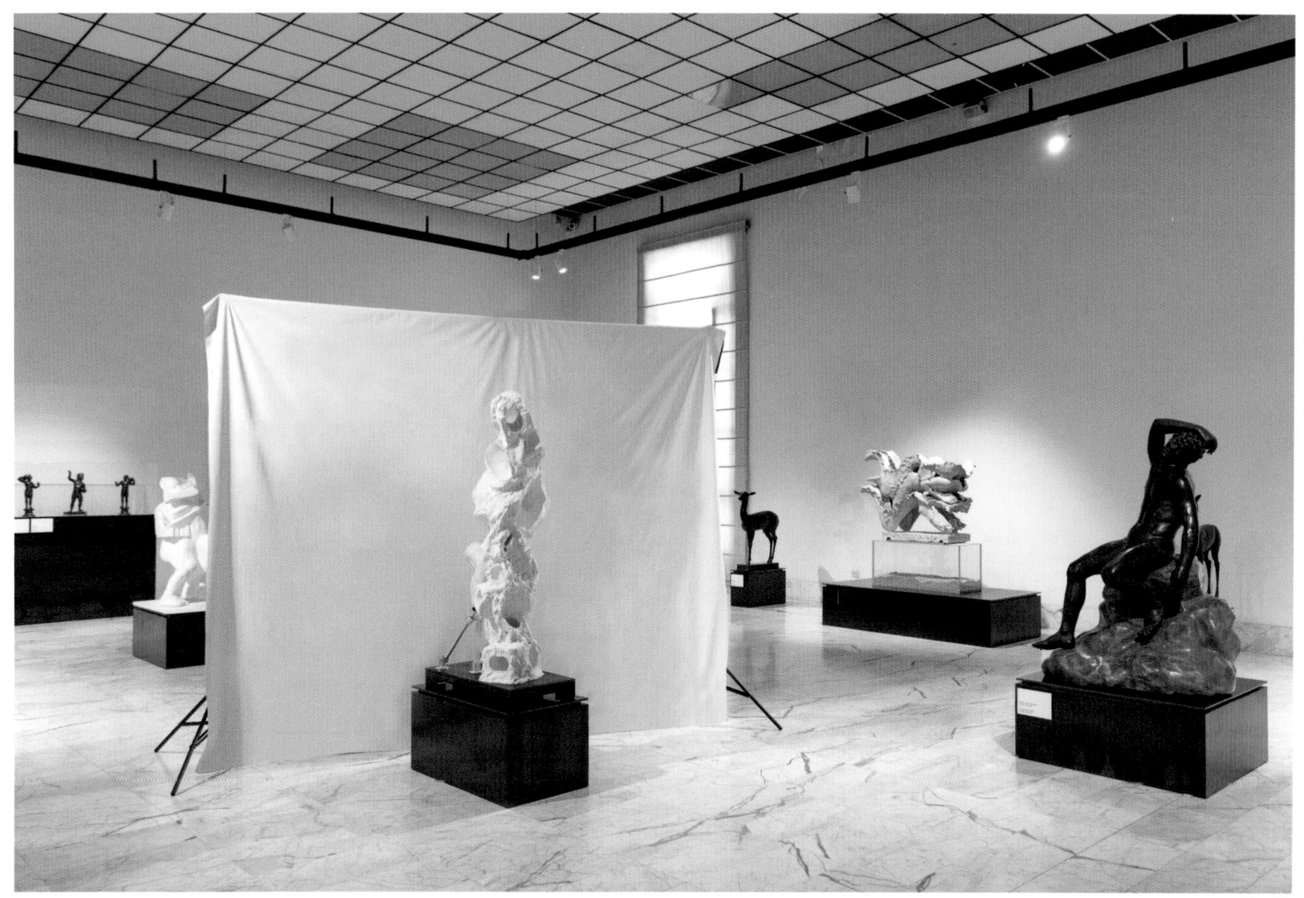

antigravitazionale, definita dalla NASA come "la posizione neutrale"; e infine la "contrazione" descritta dalla ballerina e coreografa Martha Graham.

Graham usava la "contrazione" come modo di comunicare un'emozione intensa, e i suoi ballerini si piegavano e simultaneamente utilizzavano i muscoli della parte superiore del corpo per ritrarsi in una posizione compressa.

Nella seconda teca le fotografie mostrano gruppi di ballerini, ingegneri, astronauti, archeologi nel loro ambiente di lavoro. Le immagini documentano questo impegno collettivo e la presentazione dei risultati fisici.

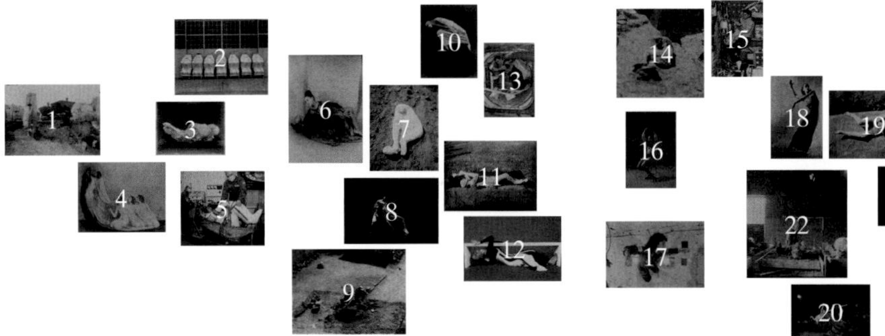

1. Workers during excavation of Pompeii Archaeological Park of Pompeii, Photographic Archive. *Addetti agli scavi a Pompei*

2. Molds for couches for test pilots at the NASA Langley Research Center's Model Workshop, 1959. *Stampi dei sedili per test pilota al Lagley Research Center Model Workshop della NASA, 1959.*

3. Plaster cast remains of Roman body (Calchi), Pompeii, late 19th- early 20th century. Archaeological Park of Pompeii, Photographic Archive. *Stampi di corpi (Calchi),Pompei, fine XIX – inizio XX secolo.*

4. Martha Graham and her first dance company, 1920's. Library of Congress Music Division, Washington DC, USA. *Martha Graham con la sua prima compagnia di danza, anni Venti.*

5. Astronaut Edward T. Lu, Russian Sokol suit leak check, The Soyuz Integration Facility at Baikonur Cosmodrome in Baikonur, Kazakhstan, 2003. Photo by NASA/Bill Ingalls. *Controlli sulla tuta russa Sokol dell'astronauta Edward T. Lu, The Soyuz Integration Facility presso Baikonur Cosmodrome in Baikonur, Kazakhstan, 2003.*

6. Martha Graham and Bertram Russell as Clytemnestra, Carl Van Vechten Trust and Library of Congress. *Martha Graham e Bertram Russell in Clitennestra.*

7. Calchi, Pompeii, late 19th- early 20th century. Archaeological Park of Pompeii, Photographic Archive. *Calchi, Pompei, fine XIX – inizio XX secolo.*

8. Martha Graham Dance Company, 'Dissonant Conversation' with CamilleBrown and Young-ha Yooo, 1989. Photo by Martha Swope, ©New York Public Library for the Performing Arts. *Martha Graham Dance Company, "Dissonant Conversation" con Camille Brown e Young-ha Yoo, 1989*

9. Workers uncovering a calchi during excavation of Pompeii, late 19th- early 20th century. Archaeological Park of Pompeii, Photographic Archive. *Addetti agli scavi scoprono un calco a Pompei tra fine XIX e inizio XX secolo*

10. Martha Graham Dance Company, 'Deep Song' with Teresa Capucilli, 1989. Photo by Martha Swope, ©New York Public Library for the Performing Arts. *Martha Graham Dance Company, "Deep Song" con Teresa Capucilli, 1989*

11. Calchi, Pompeii, late 19th- early 20th century. Archaeological Park of Pompeii, Photographic Archive. *Calchi, Pompei, fine XIX – inizio XX secolo.*

12. Martha Graham in Lamentation, Photograph by Soichi Sunami, Library of Congress Music Division, Washington DC, USA. *Martha Graham in "Lamentation".*

13. Cosmonaut Yuri I. Malenchenko, Expedition 7 mission commander sets up a video camera in the International Station, (ISS). 2003. *Il comandante della missione Expedition 7, Yuri I. Malenchenko, installa una videocamera nella Stazione Internazionale (ISS), 2003.*

14. Calchi, Pompeii, late 19th- early 20th century. Archaeological Park of Pompeii, Photographic Archive. *Calchi, Pompei, fine XIX – inizio XX secolo.*

15. Astronaut Cady Coleman works on a protein crystal growth experiement aboard the Spacelab module, NASA 1995. *L'astronauta Cady Coleman mentre lavora a un esperimento per lo sviluppo di un cristallo di proteine sullo Spacelab, NASA 1995.*

16. Martha Graham Dance Company, studio portrait of dancer Donlin Foreman in 'Circe', 1985. Photo by Martha Swope, ©New York Public Library for the Performing Arts. *Martha Graham Dance Company, ritratto del ballerino Donlin Foreman in "Circe", 1985.*

17. Astronaut Sharon Christa McAuliffe in zero-G training aboard NASA's zero gravity aircraft. Photo by NASA/Keith Meyers of the New York Times. *L'astronauta Sharon Christa McAuliffe durante un'esercitazione in assenza di gravità a bordo di un'aeromobile della NASA.*

18. Martha Graham in 'Ekstasis' (no.2), 1933. Photo by Soichi Sunami. Library of Congress, Music Division, Washington DC, USA. *Martha Graham in "Ekstasis" (no.2), 1933.*

19. Calchi Pompeii, late 19th- early 20th century. Archaeological Park of Pompeii, Photographic Archive. *Calchi, Pompei, fine XIX – inizio XX secolo.*

20. Martha Graham Dance Company production of 'Lucifer' with Janet Eilber and Rudolf Nureyev, 1975. Photo by Martha Swope ©New York Public Library for the Performing Arts. *Martha Graham Dance Company, "Lucifer" con ChJanet Eilber e Rudolf Nureyev, 1975.*

21. Astronaut Mae Jemison in Spacelab-J, 1992. NASA. *L'astronauta Mae Jemison nello Spacelab-J, 1992.*

22. Calchi Pompeii, late 19th- early 20th century. Archaeological Park of Pompeii, Photographic Archive. *Calchi, Pompei, fine XIX – inizio XX secolo*

23. Martha Graham Dance Company, 'Phaedra's Dream' with Christine Dakin and Jean-Louis Morin, 1984. Photo by Martha Swope, ©New York Public Library for the Performing Arts. *Martha Graham Dance Company, "Phaedra's Dream" con Christine Dakin e Jean-Louis Morin, 1984.*

24. Calchi, Pompeii, late 19th- early 20th century. Archaeological Park of Pompeii, Photographic Archive. *Calchi, Pompei, fine XIX – inizio XX secolo.*

25. Astronaut John B. Herrington of STS-113 works on the P1 truss of the International Space Station, NASA 2002. *L'astronauta John B. Herrington della STS-113 al lavoro sul tirante P1 dell'International Space Station, NASA 2002.*

26. Martha Graham Dance Company, 'Acts of Light', 1991. Photograph by Ruby Washington New York Times/Contrasto. *Martha Graham Dance Company, "Acts of Light", 1991.*

27. Calchi Pompeii, late 19th- early 20th century. Archaeological Park of Pompeii, Photographic Archive. *Calchi, Pompei, fine XIX – inizio XX secolo.*

28. Martha Graham in 'Cave of the Heart' (no.3), with sculptural prop by Isamu Noguchi. Library of Congress, Music Division, Washington DC, USA. *Martha Graham in "Cave of the Heart" (no.3), con oggetti di scena realizzati da Isamu Noguchi.*

29. Martha Graham Dance Company, 'Acts of Light' with Yuriko Kimura, 1984. Photo by Martha Swope, ©New York Public Library for the Performing Arts. *Martha Graham Dance Company, "Acts of Light" con Yuriko Kimura, 1984.*

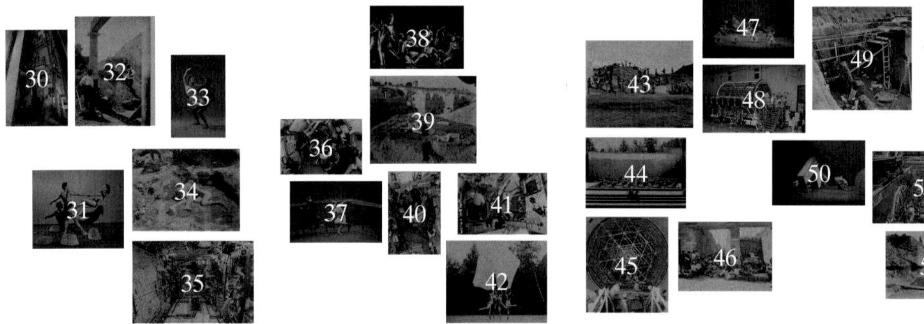

30. Technicians prepare to move the STS-133 payload at NASA's Kennedy Space Center in Florida, 2010. Photo by NASA/Dimitri Gerondidakis. *Tecnici si preparano a spostare il carico della STS-133 presso il Kennedy Space Center della NASA in Florida, 2010.*

31. Martha Graham Dance Company, 'Cave of the Heart' with Robert Cohan and Helen McGehee. Library of Congress, Washington DC, USA. *Martha Graham Dance Company, "Cave of the Heart" con Robert Cohan e Helen McGehee.*

32. Workers in the excavation of Pompeii, late 19th- early 20th century. Archaeological Park of Pompeii, Photographic Archive. *Addetti agli scavi a Pompei, fine XIX – inizio XX secolo.*

33. Martha Graham Dance Company, studio portrait of dancers Judith Garay and George White Jr. in 'Circe', 1985. Photo by Martha Swope, ©New York Public Library for the Performing Arts. *Martha Graham Dance Company, ritratto dei ballerini Judith Garay e George White Jr. in "Circe", 1985.*

34. Calchi in the excavation of Pompeii, late 19th- early 20th century. Archaeological Park of Pompeii, Photographic Archive. *Calchi negli scavi di Pompei, fine XIX – inizio XX secolo.*

35. Astronauts Terry Virts (bottom) and Scott Kelly (top) in the Destiny Laboratory performing eye exams on the ISS, 2015. *Gli astronauti Terry Virts (in basso) e Scott Kelly (in alto) nel Destiny Laboratory durante un esame alla vista a bordo del ISS, 2015.*

36. Space Shuttle Endeavour (STS-47) crew workin in the Spacelab-J module, 1992. *L'equipaggio dello Space Shuttle Endeavour (STS-47) al lavoro nel modulo Spacelab-J, 1992.*

37. Martha Graham Dance Company, 'Acrobats of God' with David Wood on barre and Helen McGehee, 1960. Photo by Martha Swope, ©New York Public Library for the Performing Arts. *Martha Graham Dance Company, "Acrobats of God" con David Wood alla sbarra e Helen McGehee, 1960.*

38. Martha Graham Dance Company, 'Eyes of the Goddess', Teresa Capucilli seated center, 1991. Photo by Martha Swope, ©New York Public Library for the Performing Arts. *Martha Graham Dance Company, "Eyes of theGoddess", Teresa Capucilli seduta al centro, 1991.*

39. Calchi in excavation of Pompeii, late 19th- early 20th century. Archaeological Park of Pompeii, Photographic Archive. *Calchi negli scavi di Pompei, fine XIX – inizio XX secolo.*

40. Cosmonaut Valery G. Korzun and STS-112 crewmembers in the Zvezda Service Module on the International Space Station. 2002. NASA. *Il cosmonauta Valery G. Korzun e i membri dell'equipaggio del STS-112 nel Zvezda Service Module sulla International Space Station, 2002.*

41. Expedition 8 and 9 crewmembers close hatch in Unity node aboard the International Space Station, 2004. NASA. *I membri dell'equipaggio delle spedizioni 8 e 9 chiudono il portello della International Space Station, 2004.*

42. Martha Graham and Denishawn Dancers in 'Soaring', 1922. Photo by Daniel Mayer, New York Public Library, Jerome Robbins Dance Division. *Martha Graham con i ballerini di Denishawn in "Soaring", 1922.*

43. Excavation of Herculaneum, late 19th- early 20th century. Archaeological Park of Pompeii, Photographic Archive. *Scavi a Ercolano, fine XIX – inizio XX secolo.*

44. Class at Denishawn School of Dancing including Martha Graham, 1923. Photo by Cutter Studio. New York Public Library, Jerome Robbins Dance Division. *Lezione alla Denishawn School of Dancing con Martha Graham, 1923.*

45. Installation of floor grids inside the Skylab Orbital Workshop, at the McDornell Douglas plant in California, NASA, 1970. *Installazione di griglie per il pavimento dello Skylab Orbital Workshop presso lo stabilimento McDornell Douglas in California, NASA, 1970.*

46. Workers resting during the excavation of Pompeii, late 19th- early 20th century. Archaeological Park of Pompeii, Photographic Archive. *Addetti ai lavori si riposano durante gli scavi di Pompei, fine XIX – inizio XX secolo.*

47. Martha Graham Dance Company, 'Adorations' 1975. Photo by Martha Swope, ©New York Public Library for the Performing Arts. *Martha Graham Dance Company, "Adorations", 1975.*

48. Kennedy Space Center, Space Station Processing Facility, Florida. NASA. *Kennedy Space Center, Space Station Processing Facility, Florida, NASA.*

49. Excavation of Herculaneum, late 19th- early 20th century. Archaeological Park of Pompeii, Photographic Archive. *Scavi a Ercolano, fine XIX – inizio XX secolo.*

50. Martha Graham Dance Company, 'Alcestis' with Martha Graham at left, 1960. Photo by Martha Swope, ©New York Public Library for the Performing Arts. *Martha Graham Dance Company, "Alcestis" con Martha Graham a sinistra, 1960.*

51. Martha Graham and her Company in 'Appalachian Spring' with set by Isamu Noguchi. Library of Congress, Washington DC, USA, Music Division. *Martha Graham con la sua compagnia in "Appalachian Spring" con set di isamu Noguchi.*

52. The International Space Station ground crew deliver the Integrated Truss Structure in a ceremony at the Space Station Processing Facility, Kennedy Space Center, Florida, 2000. NASA. *L'equipaggio a terra della International Space Station consegna la Integrated Truss Structure nel corso di una cerimonia presso la Space Station Processing Facility, Kennedy Space Center, Florida, 2000.*

53. Orbiter Processing Facility 2 at NASA's Kennedy Space Center, Florida. The STS-134 crew and technicians check out space shuttle Endeavour's payload bay, 2011. Photo by NASA/Frankie Martin. *Orbiter Processing Facility 2, Kennedy Space Center della NASA, Florida. L'equipaggio e i tecnici della STS-134 controllano la piattaforma per il carico dell'Endeavour, 2011.*

54. Excavation of Herculaneum, late 19th- early 20th century. Archaeological Park of Pompeii, Photographic Archive. *Scavi a Ercolano, fine XIX – inizio XX secolo.*

55. Military visitors to excavation of Pompeii, late 19th- early 20th century. Archaeological Park of Pompeii, Photographic Archive. *Militari visitano gli scavi di Pompei, fine XIX – inizio XX secolo.*

56. Martha Graham Dance Company, 'Cortege of Eagles' with Bertram Ross (lying down at rear) and Martha Graham (right), 1967. Photo by Martha Swope, ©New York Public Library for the Performing Arts. *Martha Graham Dance Company, "Cortege of Eagles" con Bertram Ross (sdraiato dietro) e Martha Graham (a destra), 1967.*

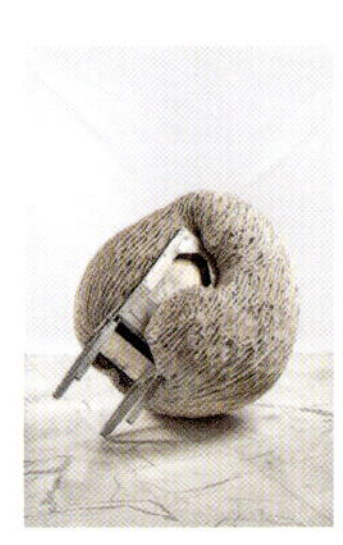

Anthropometry
Antropometria
2019

Aquaresin, aluminum, steel, clay.
Acquaresina, alluminio, acciaio, argilla

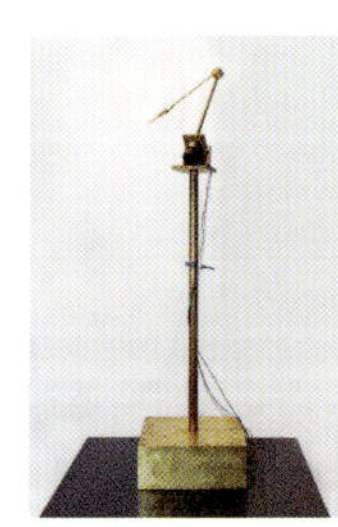

Atlas
Atlante
2019

Brass, rotation motor, Neolithic Dalton point, electronics, wood.
Ottone, motore rotante, punta di lancia neolitica, componenti elettroniche, legno.

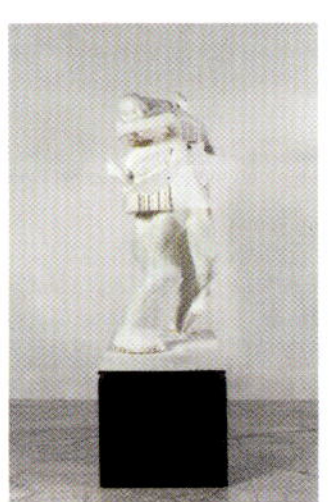

Species-specific_005
Specie-specifico_005
2019

3D printed PLA, supports.
PLA stampato in 3D, supporti.

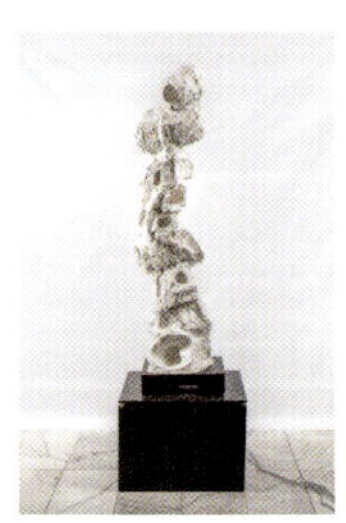

Contraction 1
Contrazione 1
2019

Plaster, steel.
Gesso, acciaio.

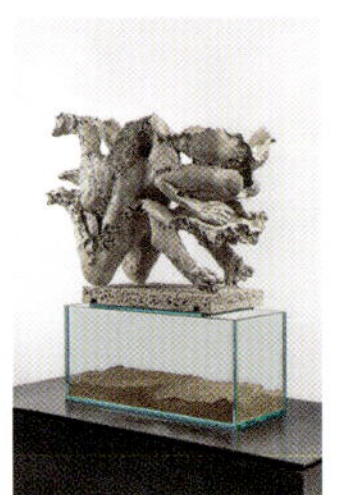

Calcify
Calcificare
2019

Aquaresin, Hydrocal, glass fiber, steel, clay, pigment, glass, sand.
Acquaresina, Hydrocal, fibra di vetro, acciaio, argilla, pigmenti, vetro, sabbia.

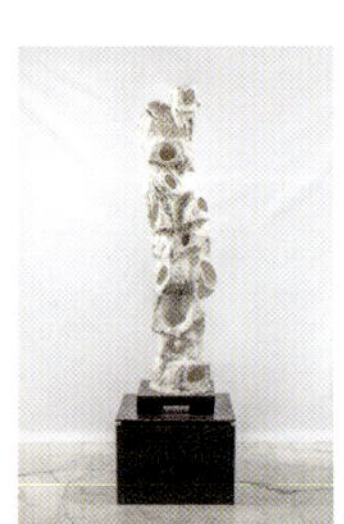

Contraction 2
Contrazione 2
2019

Plaster, steel.
Gesso, acciaio.

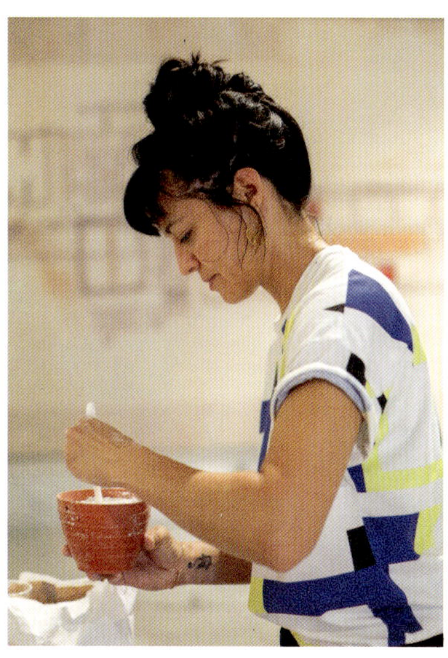

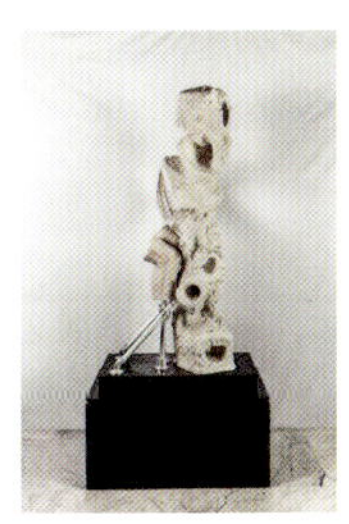

Contraction 3
Contrazione 3
2019

Plaster, steel.
Gesso, acciaio.

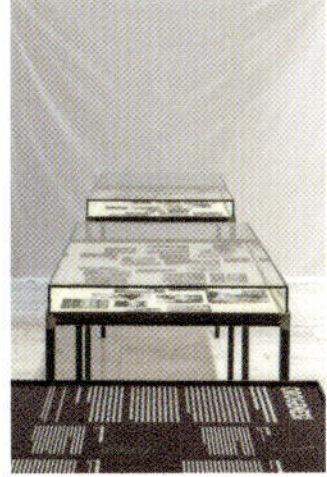

Attitude 1 & 2
Attitude 1 & 2
2019

Archival photographs, steel and glass display.
Fotografie d'archivio, alluminio e teca di vetro.

Juliana Cerqueira Leite is a Brazilian sculptor based in New York. Her artworks in sculpture, photography and video navigate the history, contexts and possible futures of representing the human form. She was awarded a Pollock-Krasner Foundation Grant in 2019, and in 2016 she was awarded the Furla Art Prize for her contribution to the 5th Moscow Young Art Biennale. Leite has exhibited her work in group shows internationally, including the Sculpture Center, (New York), Saatchi Gallery (London), the Venice Biennale Antarctic Pavilion, the Vancouver Sculpture Biennale, Kunsthaus Erfurt, Marres House for Contemporary Culture (Maastricht, NL) and Hordaland Kunstsenter for the 2019 Bergen Assembly. She has exhibited her work in solo shows including Instituto Tomie Ohtake (São Paulo), T.J. Boulting Gallery (London), Alma Zevi (Venice), Galeria Casa Triângulo (São Paulo), Regina Rex and Arsenal Contemporary (New York). Leite graduated from the Slade School of Fine Art MFA in London in 2006, as recipient of the Kenneth Armitage Sculpture Prize. She is represented by Alma Zevi, TJ Boulting and Casa Triângulo galleries.

ACKNOWLEDGEMENTS
RINGRAZIAMENTI

This exhibition began with a deep respect for the formative and sustained influence that the objects preserved within the National Archaeological Museum in Naples (MANN) have had on contemporary ideas about democracy, patriarchy, nature and progress.

The production of Orogenesis was funded by a Pollock-Krasner Foundation Grant, the support of Alma Zevi gallery and the Juliana Cerqueira Leite Exhibition Circle.

I am grateful for the continued support and encouragement from colleagues, family and friends:

Alma Zevi who as my gallery director and friend carried the torch of this idea, and through two years of challenges and persistence, made it so this exhibition could be possible; Nadim Samman, for encouraging the concept of presenting this new body of work at MANN and following its progress with curatorial feedback and friendship; Michele Iodice for his elegant vision, support and logistical expertise as our curator and main advocate in Naples; Paolo Giulierini for his expansive leadership as director of MANN, and to the staff of MANN for their generosity in opening their doors to us; Mario Codognato for his invaluable support in recommending our project, his insights and generous introduction in this catalogue; Dehlia Hannah for her rigorous thinking and ability to transform concepts into words; the inimitable Jodie Petrosino and Teresa Fico of Lending Art for their elegant assistance with the logistics of this international production; Beatrice Orlandi whose uniquely heterogeneous skills made this project reach further than I could have imagined; Federica Cavazzuti for her graceful translations into Italian and steadfast multi-faceted support; Raffaela Naldi-Rossano for her generous Neapolitan hospitality, her community-building friendship and late night conversations; the support of Residency 80121; Valeria Casaforte and La Casaforte S.B. for their support and for the beautiful workspace in Naples; Professor Steven Dubowsky and Elena Flynn for their generosity, time and expertise in the design and production of 'Atlas'; Rodrigo Editore and Casa Triângulo in São Paulo; Fonderia Nolana; Michele Borgongino and the Parco Archeologico di Pompeii; Meredith Glisson for her patience with my directions and her movements in 'Species-Specific'; em eterna gratidão à minha família pelo seu amor e apoio.

This publication owes much to the leadership of my gallery director, publisher and friend Hannah Watson of Trolley Books and TJ Boulting gallery, and the vision of Emma Scott-Child and Junction Studio. Thanks also to the support of Victoria Thomas and Darryl de Prez, and Janine Ulfane.

With a very special thanks to Olivier and Desiree Berggruen without whose nurturing encouragement and support this catalogue would not have been possible.

In memory of a beautiful friend, visionary artist and thinker Sascha Pohflepp (1978-2019), who cheered me on through the production of this exhibition and body of work, and is in my heart as it extends into the future.

Photographs - © Enrico Fiorese, Amedeo Benestante

Text - © Mario Codognato, Nadim Samman & Dehlia Hannah

Translation - Federica Cavazzuti, Lucia Longhi

Design - Emma Scott-Child

A catalogue record for this book is available from the British Library

ISBN 978-1-907112-62-1

Printed in Italy 2019 by Grafiche Antiga
Published in Great Britain in 2019 by Trolley Ltd

www.trolleybooks.com

TROLLEY

M museo archeologico nazionale di napoli

Cut - ^{cm}

2× - 5.7cm (2×3)

-36.6cm

-36.9cm

4 × 177.6 cm